DYNAMIC

FREEDOMS

Compiled by

WILLIAM G. SIZEMORE, 33°
(Rear Admiral, U.S. Navy, Retired)
Director of Education and Americanism

THE SUPREME COUNCIL, 33°

Ancient and Accepted Scottish Rite of Freemasonry
Southern Jurisdiction, U.S.A.
Mother Supreme Council of the World
1733 16th Street, NW, Washington, DC 20009

TABLE OF CONTENTS

First Edition, 1977 . . . . .475,000 copies
Second Printing, July 1981 . . . . .25,000 copies
Third Printing, August 1982 . . . . .25,000 copies
Fourth Printing, February 1983 . . . . .10,000 copies
Fifth Printing, September 1983 . . . . .25,000 copies
Sixth Printing, June 1984 . . . . .25,000 copies
Second Edition, October 1986 . . . . .10,000 copies
Third Edition, October 1987 . . . . .25,000 copies

Back cover: National Geographic Society Photographer
Courtesy U.S. Capitol Historical Society

FOREWORD

Truth is forever, and there is no greater truth than that man must be free. The documents presented in this book capture moments in the history of America when our forebears took giant steps toward liberty. By preserving this living record of our Nation's past, the Scottish Rite brings to every new generation the principles of freedom that, as Thomas Jefferson said, "form the bright constellation which has guided our steps through an age of revolution and transformation."

Today, too, is "an age of revolution and transformation." It is necessary now as it was over two centuries ago to understand and fight for the ideals that carried America to independence and that still keep us free today. The political rights and civil liberties of 42 percent of the world's population are severely limited or totally repressed. Unless Americans remember and preserve our rich heritage of liberty, a new Dark Age of tyranny could lock the majority of mankind into the harsh chains of totalitarian slavery.

The choice is ours. We are free. Given the action of good men, we will remain free. No society is stronger than the sum of its individual citizens. Consequently, the Scottish Rite is dedicated to making good men better, to building each individual's inner temple of moral character and spiritual achievement. And freedom in all its forms—speech, press, assembly, petition, religion—is essential to this work.

As you read and reread these pages, make this book more than a part of your personal library—make it a part of your life.

C Fred Kleinknecht

Sovereign Grand Commander

OUR
FREEDOM
DOCUMENTS

THE MAGNA CARTA

T HE liberties we enjoy didn't suddenly spring into being. They were developed and fought for over long periods of time. And the Magna Carta, or Great Charter, was the first step toward constitutional liberty for all people of the English-speaking world. It was signed by King John in 1215.

At that time, no one dreamed that this step was laying the foundations for a new kind of government. The nobles who forced the king to sign it were only concerned with their own welfare. What had happened in England was that the kings had begun to unify the country. As they took over more and more power, the feudal lords and barons felt they were losing their special privileges.

UNREST

At the time of King John, there was much unrest in the land and the nobles saw a chance to get back some of their privileges. So they drew up a list of their demands about the old rights they wanted back. The king twice refused to consider them. But when the barons gathered an army to oppose the king, he had no choice but to sign the Magna Carta on June 15, 1215.

While the nobles thought chiefly of themselves, they also promised certain rights to the freemen under their control. It was the first document that promised specific rights to all freemen in the nation.

The original Magna Carta had 63 articles, and three of those articles have importance for us today. One declares that no freeman shall be deprived of his life or property without a verdict of his equals or by the law of the land.

JUSTICE

Another article states that justice shall not be sold, denied or delayed. And a third section provides that taxes cannot be levied without the consent of the barons.

So you can see how life, property, justice, taxes, are all being considered in a new way, a way that is practiced by our government today.

While the Magna Carta was really not concerned with democracy, it was a major step forward in the development of freedom. It meant there was a law which was above the king and which he could not break. **(Reprinted by permission of the Washington Star).**

KING JOHN SIGNING MAGNA CARTA

THE MAYFLOWER COMPACT

November 11, 1620

IN THE NAME OF GOD, AMEN. We whose names are under-written, the Loyal Subjects of our dread Sovereign Lord King *James,* by the Grace of God, of *Great Britain, France,* and *Ireland,* King, *Defender of the Faith,* &c. Having undertaken, for the Glory of God, and Advancement of the Christian Faith, and Honour of our King and Country, a Voyage to plant the first Colony in the northern Parts of *Virginia;* Do by these Presents solemnly and mutually in the Presence of God, and one another, covenant and combine ourselves together into a civil Body Politick, for our better Ordering and Preservation and Furtherance of the Ends aforesaid; And by Virtue hereof to enact, constitute, and frame such just and equal Laws, Ordinances, Acts, Constitutions, and Officers, from time to time, as shall be thought most meet and convenient for the general Good of the Colony; unto which we promise all due Submission and Obedience. IN WITNESS whereof we have hereunder subscribed our names at *Cape-Cod* the eleventh of *November,* in the year of the Reign of our Sovereign Lord, King *James,* of *England, France,* and *Ireland,* the eighteenth and of *Scotland,* the fifty-fourth, *Anno Domini,* 1620.

(The original list of signers has disappeared. Nathaniel Morton, writing in 1669, listed forty-one signers of the document. Channing, Edward, A History of the United States, 6 vols., 1928, I, chap. 11.)

THE CALL TO ARMS

PATRICK HENRY
1775

MR. PRESIDENT, it is natural to man to indulge in the illusions of hope. We are apt to shut our eyes against a painful truth. Is this the part of wise men, engaged in a great and arduous struggle for liberty? Are we disposed to be of the number of those, who, having eyes, see not, and having ears, hear not, the things which so nearly concern their temporal salvation? For my part, whatever anguish of spirit it may cost, I am willing to know the whole truth; to know the worst, and to provide for it.

I have but one lamp by which my feet are guided; and that is the lamp of experience. I know of no way of judging of the future but by the past. Let us not, I beseech you, sir, deceive ourselves longer. Sir, we have done everything that could be done to avert the storm which is now coming on. We have petitioned; we have remonstrated; we have supplicated; we have prostrated ourselves before the throne, and have implored its interposition to arrest the tyrannical hands of the ministry and Parliament. Our petitions have been slighted; our remonstrances have produced additional violence and insult; our supplications have been disregarded; and we have been spurned, with contempt, from the foot of the throne! In vain, after these things, may we indulge the fond hope of peace and reconciliation. There is no longer any room for hope. If we wish to be free— if we mean to preserve inviolate those inestimable privileges for which we have been so long contending—if we mean not basely to abandon the noble struggle in which we have been so long engaged, and which we have pledged ourselves never to abandon, until the glorious object of our contest shall be obtained—we must fight! I repeat it, sir, we must fight! An appeal to arms and to the God of Hosts is all that is left us!

They tell us, sir, that we are weak—unable to cope with so formidable an adversary. But when shall we be stronger? Will it be the next week, or the next year? Will it be when we are totally disarmed? Shall we acquire the means of effectual resistance by lying supinely on our backs and hugging the delusive phantom of hope, until our enemies shall have bound us hand and foot?

Sir, we are not weak if we make a proper use of those means which the God of nature has placed in our power. Three millions of people armed in the holy cause of liberty, and in such a country as

PATRICK HENRY
1736 - 1799

THE CALL TO ARMS

that which we possess, are invincible by any force which our enemy can send against us. Besides, sir, we shall not fight our battles alone. There is a just God who presides over the destines of nations, and who will raise up friends to fight our battles for us. The battle, sir, is not to the strong alone; it is to the vigilant, the active, the brave.

It is in vain, sir, to extenuate the matter. Gentleman may cry "Peace, peace"—But there is no peace. The war is actually begun! Our brethren are already in the field! Why stand we here idle? What is it that gentlemen wish? What would they have? Is life so dear, or peace so sweet, as to be purchased at the price of chains and slavery? Forbid it, Almighty God! I know not what course others may take; but as for me, give me liberty or give me death!

Every tomorrow has two handles. You can take hold of tomorrow with the handle of anxiety or you can take hold of it with the handle of faith.

—Henry Ward Beecher

THE GREATEST BELL IN THE WORLD

The Liberty Bell as it appears today in Independence Hall, Philadelphia, Pa. The circumference around the lip is 12 feet; around the crown, 7 feet 6 inches. From lip to crown measures 3 feet, and the clapper is 3 feet 2 inches long. The metal is 3 inches thick at the lip, and the over-all weight is 2080 pounds.

THE DECLARATION OF INDEPENDENCE

IN CONGRESS, JULY 4, 1776

W HEN in the Course of human events, it becomes necessary for one people to dissolve the political bands which have connected them with another, and to assume among the powers of the earth, the separate and equal station to which the Laws of Nature and of Nature's God entitle them, a decent respect to the opinions of mankind requires that they should declare the causes which impel them to the separation.

We hold these truths to be self-evident, that all men are created equal, that they are endowed by their Creator with certain unalienable Rights, that among these are Life, Liberty and the pursuit of Happiness. That to secure these rights, Governments are instituted among Men, deriving their just powers from the consent of the governed. That whenever any Form of Government becomes destructive of these ends, it is the Right of the People to alter or to abolish it, and to institute new Government, laying its foundation on such principles and organizing its powers in such form, as to them shall seem most likely to effect their Safety and Happiness. Prudence, indeed, will dictate that Governments long established should not be changed for light and transient causes; and accordingly all experience hath shewn that mankind are more disposed to suffer, while evils are sufferable, than to right themselves by abolishing the forms to which they are accustomed. But when a long train of abuses and usurpations, pursuing invariably the same Object evinces a design to reduce them under absolute Despotism, it is their right, it is their duty, to throw off such Government, and to provide new Guards for their future security. Such has been the patient sufferance of these Colonies; and such is now the necessity which constrains them to alter their former Systems of Government. The history of the present King of Great Britain is a history of repeated injuries and usurpations, all having in direct object the establishment of an absolute Tyranny over these States. To prove this, let Facts be submitted to a candid world.

He has refused his Assent to Laws, the most wholesome and necessary for the public good. He has forbidden his Governors to pass Laws of immediate and pressing importance, unless suspended in their operation till his Assent should be obtained; and when so suspended, he has utterly neglected to attend to them.

He has refused to pass other Laws for the accommodation of large districts of people, unless those people would relinquish the right of Representation in the Legislature, a right inestimable to them and formidable to tyrants only.

He has called together legislative bodies at places unusual, uncomfortable, and distant from the depository of their public Records, for the sole purpose of fatiguing them into compliance with his measures.

He has dissolved Representative Houses repeatedly, for opposing with manly firmness his invasions on the rights of the people.

He has refused for a long time, after such dissolutions, to cause others to be elected; whereby the Legislative powers, incapable of Annihilation, have returned to the People at large for their exercise; the State remaining in the meantime exposed to all the dangers of invasion from without, and convulsions within.

He has endeavored to prevent the population of these States; for that purpose obstructing the Laws of Naturalization of Foreigners; refusing to pass others to encourage their migrations hither, and raising the conditions of new Appropriations of Lands.

He has obstructed the Administration of Justice, by refusing his Assent to Laws for establishing Judiciary Powers.

He has made Judges dependent on his Will alone, for the tenure of their offices, and the amount and payment of their salaries.

He has erected a multitude of New Offices, and sent hither swarms of Officers to harass our people, and eat out their substance.

He has kept among us, in times of peace, Standing Armies without the Consent of our legislatures.

He has affected to render the Military independent of and superior to the Civil power.

He has combined with others to subject us to a jurisdiction foreign to our constitution, and unacknowledged by our laws; giving his Assent to their Acts of pretended Legislation: For quartering large bodies of armed troops among us: For protecting them, by a mock Trial, from punishment for any Murders which they should commit on the Inhabitants of these States: For cutting off our Trade with all parts of the world: For imposing Taxes on us without our

Consent: For depriving us in many cases, of the benefits of Trial by Jury: For transporting us beyond Seas to be tried for pretended offences: For abolishing the free System of English Laws in a neighbouring Province, establishing therein an Arbitrary government, and enlarging its Boundaries so as to render it at once an example and fit instrument for introducing the same absolute rule into these Colonies: For taking away our Charters, abolishing our most valuable Laws, and altering fundamentally the Forms of our Governments: For suspending our own Legislatures, and declaring themselves invested with power to legislate for us in all cases whatsoever.

He has abdicated Government here, by declaring us out of his Protection and waging War against us.

He has plundered our seas, ravaged our Coasts, burnt our towns, and destroyed the lives of our people.

He is at this time transporting large Armies of foreign Mercenaries to complete the works of death, desolation and tyranny, already begun with circumstances of Cruelty & perfidy scarcely paralleled in the most barbarous ages, and totally unworthy the Head of a civilized nation.

He has constrained our fellow Citizens taken Captive on the high Seas to bear Arms against their Country, to become the executioners of their friends and Brethren, or to fall themselves by their Hands.

He has excited domestic insurrections amongst us, and has endeavored to bring on the inhabitants of our frontiers, the merciless Indian Savages, whose known rule of warfare, is an undistinguished destruction of all ages, sexes and conditions.

In every stage of these Oppressions We have Petitioned for Redress in the most humble terms: Our repeated Petitions have been answered only by repeated injury. A Prince, whose character is thus marked by every act which may define a Tyrant, is unfit to be the ruler of a free people. Nor have We been wanting in attentions to our British brethren. We have warned them from time to time of attempts by their legislature to extend an unwarrantable jurisdiction over us. We have reminded them of the circumstances of our emigration and settlement here. We have appealed to their native justice and magnanimity, and we have conjured them by the ties of our common kindred to disavow these usurpations, which would inevitably interrupt our connections and correspondence. They too have been deaf to the voice of justice and of consanguinity. We must, therefore, acquiesce in the necessity, which denounces our Separation, and hold them, as we hold the rest of mankind, Enemies in War, in Peace, Friends.

WE THEREFORE, the Representatives of the UNITED STATES OF AMERICA, in General Congress, Assembled, appealing to the Supreme Judge of the world for the rectitude of our intentions, do, in the Name, and by Authority of the Good People of these Colonies, solemnly publish and declare, That these United Colonies are, and of Right ought to be FREE AND INDEPENDENT STATES; that they are Absolved from all Allegiance to the British Crown, and that all political connection between them and the State of Great Britain, is and ought to be totally dissolved; and that as Free and Independent States, they have full Power to levy War, conclude Peace, contract Alliances, establish Commerce, and to do all other Acts and Things which Independent States may of right do. And for the support of this Declaration, with a firm reliance on the protection of Divine Providence, we mutually pledge to each other our Lives, our Fortunes and our sacred Honor.

THOMAS JEFFERSON
1743 - 1826

Author of the Declaration of Independence

The Shrine Containing the
Declaration of Independence
and the
Constitution of the United States
of America.

17

THE CONSTITUTION OF THE UNITED STATES OF AMERICA

PREAMBLE

WE THE PEOPLE of the United States, in Order to form a more perfect Union, establish Justice, insure domestic Tranquility, provide for the common defense, promote the general Welfare, and secure the Blessings of Liberty to ourselves and our Posterity, do ordain and establish this Constitution for the United States of America.

ARTICLE I

SECTION 1

Legislative powers vested in Congress

All legislative Powers herein granted shall be vested in a Congress of the United States, which shall consist of a Senate and House of Representatives.

SECTION 2

Composition of the House of Representatives

1. The House of Representatives shall be composed of Members chosen every second Year by the People of the several States, and the Electors in each State shall have the Qualifications requisite for Electors of the most numerous Branch of the State Legislature.

Qualification of Representatives

2. No Person shall be a Representative who shall not have attained to the Age of twenty-five Years, and been seven Years a Citizen of the United States, and who shall not, when elected, be an Inhabitant of that State in which he shall be chosen.

Apportionment of Representatives and direct taxes—census*

3. [Representatives and direct Taxes shall be apportioned among the several States which may be included within this Union, according to their respective Numbers, which shall be determined by adding to the whole Number of free Persons, including those bound to Service for

The clause included in brackets is amended by the 14th Amendment, Section 2.

18

a Term of Years, and excluding Indians not taxed, three fifths of all other Persons.] The actual Enumeration shall be made within three Years after the first Meeting of the Congress of the United States, and within every subsequent Term of ten Years, in such Manner as they shall by Law direct. The Number of Representatives shall not exceed one for every thirty Thousand, but each State shall have at Least one Representative; and until such enumeration shall be made, the State of New Hampshire shall be entitled to chuse three, Massachusetts eight, Rhode Island and Providence Plantations one, Connecticut five, New York six, New Jersey four, Pennsylvania eight, Delaware one, Maryland six, Virginia ten, North Carolina five, South Carolina five, and Georgia three.

Filling of vacancies in representation

4. When vacancies happen in the Representation from any State, the Executive Authority thereof shall issue Writs of Election to fill such Vacancies.

Selection of officers; power of impeachment

5. The House of Representatives shall chuse their Speaker and other Officers; and shall have the sole Power of Impeachment.

The Senate

SECTION 3†

[1. The Senate of the United States shall be composed of two Senators from each State, chosen by the Legislature thereof, for six Years; and each Senator shall have one Vote.]

Classification of Senators; filling of vacancies

2. Immediately after they shall be assembled in Consequence of the first Election, they shall be divided as equally as may be into three Classes. The Seats of the Senators of the first Class shall be vacated at the Expiration of the second Year, of the second Class at the Expiration of the fourth Year, and of the third Class at the Expiration of the sixth Year, so that one-third may be chosen every second Year; and if Vacancies happen by Resignation, or otherwise, during the Recess of the Legislature of any State, the Executive thereof may make temporary Appointments [until the next Meeting of the Legislature, which shall then fill such Vacancies].

---

† *The 1st paragraph of this section and as much of the 2nd paragraph as relates to filling vacancies are amended by the 17th Amendment.*

Qualification of Senators

3. No Person shall be a Senator who shall not have attained the Age of thirty Years, and been nine Years a Citizen of the United States, and who shall not, when elected, be an Inhabitant of that State for which he shall be chosen.

Vice President to be President of Senate

4. The Vice President of the United States shall be President of the Senate, but shall have no Vote, unless they be equally divided.

Selection of Senate officers; President pro tempore

5. The Senate shall chuse their other Officers, and also a President pro tempore, in the Absence of the Vice President, or when he shall exercise the Office of President of the United States.

Senate to try impeachments

6. The Senate shall have the sole Power to try all Impeachments. When sitting for that Purpose, they shall be on Oath or Affirmation. When the President of the United States is tried, the Chief Justice shall preside: And no Person shall be convicted without the Concurrence of two thirds of the Members present.

Judgment in cases of impeachment

7. Judgment in Cases of Impeachment shall not extend further than to removal from Office, and disqualification to hold and enjoy any Office of honor, Trust or Profit under the United States: but the Party convicted shall nevertheless be liable and subject to Indictment, Trial, Judgment and Punishment, according to Law.

SECTION 4

Control of congressional elections

1. The Times, Places and Manner of holding Elections for Senators and Representatives, shall be prescribed in each State by the Legislature thereof; but the Congress may at any time by Law make or alter such Regulations, except as to the Places of chusing Senators.

Time for assembling of Congress†

2. The Congress shall assemble at least once in every Year, and such Meeting shall be on the first Monday in December, unless they shall by Law appoint a different Day.

---

† *Amended by the 20th Amendment, Section 2.*

THE CONSTITUTION OF THE UNITED STATES

SECTION 5

Each house to be the judge of the election and qualifications of its members; regulations as to quorum

1. Each House shall be the Judge of the Elections, Returns and Qualifications of its own Members, and a Majority of each shall constitute a Quorum to do Business; but a smaller Number may adjourn from day to day, and may be authorized to compel the Attendance of absent Members, in such Manner, and under such Penalties as each House may provide.

Each house to determine its own rules

2. Each House may determine the Rules of its Proceedings, punish its Members for disorderly Behaviour, and, with the Concurrence of two thirds, expel a Member.

Journals and yeas and nays

3. Each House shall keep a Journal of its Proceedings, and from time to time publish the same, excepting such Parts as may in their Judgment require Secrecy; and the Yeas and Nays of the Members of either House on any question shall, at the Desire of one fifth of those Present, be entered on the Journal.

Adjournment

4. Neither House, during the Session of Congress shall, without the Consent of the other, adjourn for more than three days, nor to any other Place than that in which the two Houses shall be sitting.

SECTION 6

Compensation and privileges of Members of Congress

1. The Senators and Representatives shall receive a Compensation for their Services, to be ascertained by Law, and paid out of the Treasury of the United States. They shall in all Cases, except Treason, Felony and Breach of the Peace, be privileged from Arrest during their Attendance at the Session of their respective Houses, and in going to and returning from the same; and for any Speech or Debate in either House, they shall not be questioned in any other Place.

Incompatable offices; exclusions

2. No Senator or Representative shall, during the Time for which he was elected, be appointed to any civil Office under the Authority of

the United States, which shall have been created, or the Emoluments whereof shall have been encreased during such time; and no Person holding any Office under the United States, shall be a Member of either House during his Continuance of Office.

SECTION 7

Revenue bills to originate in House

1. All Bills for raising Revenue shall originate in the House of Representatives; but the Senate may propose or concur with Amendments as on other Bills.

Manner of passing bills; veto power of President

2. Every Bill which shall have passed the House of Representatives and the Senate, shall, before it becomes a Law, be presented to the President of the United States; If he approve he shall sign it, but if not he shall return it, with his Objections to that House in which it shall have originated, who shall enter the Objections at large on their Journal, and proceed to reconsider it. If after such Reconsideration two thirds of that House shall agree to pass the Bill, it shall be sent, together with the Objections, to the other House, by which it shall likewise be reconsidered, and if approved by two thirds of that House, it shall become a Law. But in all such Cases the Votes of both Houses shall be determined by Yeas and Nays, and the Names of the Persons voting for and against the Bill shall be entered on the Journal of each House respectively. If any Bill shall not be returned by the President within ten Days (Sundays excepted) after it shall have been presented to him, the Same shall be a Law, in like Manner as if he had signed it, unless the Congress by their Adjournment prevents its Return, in which Case it shall not be a Law.

Concurrent orders or resolutions, to be passed by President

3. Every Order, Resolution, or Vote to which the Concurrence of the Senate and House of Representatives may be necessary (except on a question of Adjournment) shall be presented to the President of the United States; and before the Same shall take Effect, shall be approved by him, or being disapproved by him, shall be repassed by two thirds of the Senate and House of Representatives, according to the Rules and Limitations prescribed in the Case of a Bill.

THE CONSTITUTION OF THE UNITED STATES

SECTION 8

General powers of Congress

The Congress shall have Power.—1. To lay and collect Taxes, Duties, Imposts and Excises, to pay the Debts and provide for the common Defense and general Welfare of the United States; but all Duties, Imposts and Excises shall be uniform throughout the United States;

Borrowing of money

2. To borrow Money on the credit of the United States;

Regulation of commerce

3. To regulate Commerce with foreign Nations, and among the several States, and with the Indian Tribes;

Naturalization and bankruptcy

4. To establish an uniform Rule of Naturalization, and uniform Laws on the subject of Bankruptcies throughout the United States;

Money, weights and measures

5. To coin Money, regulate the Value thereof, and of foreign Coin, and fix the Standard of Weights and Measures;

Counterfeiting

6. To provide for the Punishment of counterfeiting the Securities and current Coin of the United States;

Post offices

7. To establish Post Offices and post Roads;

Patents and copyrights

8. To promote the Progress of Science and useful Arts, by securing for limited Times to Authors and Inventors the exclusive Right to their respective Writings and Discoveries;

Inferior courts

9. To constitute Tribunals inferior to the supreme Court;

Piracies and felonies

10. To define and punish Piracies and Felonies committed on the high Seas, and Offences against the Law of Nations;

War; marque and reprisal

11. To declare War, grant Letters of Marque and Reprisal, and make Rules concerning Captures on Land and Water;

Armies

12. To raise and support Armies, but no Appropriation of Money to that Use shall be for a longer Term than two Years;

Navy

13. To provide and maintain a Navy;

Land and naval forces

14. To make Rules for the Government and Regulation of the land and naval Forces;

Calling out militia

15. To provide for calling forth the Militia to execute the Laws of the Union, suppress Insurrections and repel Invasions;

Organizing, arming and disciplining militia

16. To provide for organizing, arming, and disciplining, the Militia, and for governing such Part of them as may be employed in the Service of the United States, reserving to the States respectively, the Appointment of the Officers, and the Authority of training the Militia according to the discipline prescribed by Congress;

Exclusive legislation over District of Columbia

17. To exercise exclusive Legislation in all Cases whatsoever, over such District (not exceeding ten Miles square) as may, by Cession of particular States, and the Acceptance of Congress, become the Seat of the Government of the United States, and to exercise like Authority over all Places purchased by the Consent of the Legislature of the State in which the Same shall be, for the Erection of Forts, Magazines, Arsenals, dock-Yards, and other needful Buildings;—And

To enact laws necessary to enforce Constitution

18. To make all Laws which shall be necessary and proper for carrying into Execution the foregoing Powers, and all other Powers vested by this Constitution in the Government of the United States, or in any Department or Officer thereof.

SECTION 9

Migration or importation of certain persons not to be prohibited before 1808

1. The Migration or Importation of such Persons as any of the States now existing shall think proper to admit, shall not be prohibited by the Congress prior to the Year one thousand eight hundred and eight, but a Tax or duty may be imposed on such Importation, not exceeding ten dollars for each Person.

Writ of habeas corpus not to be suspended; exception

2. The Privilege of the Writ of Habeas Corpus shall not be suspended, unless when in Cases of Rebellion or Invasion the public Safety may require it.

Bills of attainder and ex post facto laws prohibited

3. No Bill of Attainder or ex post facto Law shall be passed.

Capitation and other direct taxes

4. No Capitation, or other direct, Tax shall be laid, unless in Proportion to the Census or Enumeration herein before directed to be taken.*

Exports not to be taxed

5. No Tax or Duty shall be laid on Articles exported from any State.

No preference to be given to ports of any State; interstate shipping

6. No Preference shall be given by any Regulation of Commerce or Revenue to the Ports of one State over those of another: nor shall Vessels bound to, or from, one State, be obliged to enter, clear, or pay Duties in another.

Money, how drawn from treasury; financial statements to be published

7. No Money shall be drawn from the Treasury, but in Consequence of Appropriations made by law; and a regular Statement and Account of the Receipts and Expenditures of all public Money shall be published from time to time.

---

* See the 16th Amendment.

Titles of nobility not to be granted; acceptance by government officers of favors from foreign powers

8. No Title of Nobility shall be granted by the United States: And no Person holding any Office of Profit or Trust under them, shall, without the Consent of the Congress, accept of any present, Emolument, Office, or Title, of any kind whatever, from any King, Prince, or foreign State.

SECTION 10

Limitations of the powers of the several States

1. No State shall enter into any Treaty, Alliance, or Confederation; grant Letters of Marque and Reprisal; coin Money; emit Bills of Credit; make any Thing but gold and silver Coin a Tender in Payment of Debts; pass any Bill of Attainder, ex post facto Law, or Law impairing the Obligation of Contracts, or grant any Title of Nobility.

State imposts and duties

2. No State shall, without the Consent of the Congress, lay any Imposts or Duties on Imports or Exports, except what may be absolutely necessary for executing its inspection Laws: and the net Produce of all Duties and Imposts, laid by any State on Imports or Exports, shall be for the Use of the Treasury of the United States; and all such Laws shall be subject to the Revision and Control of the Congress.

Further restrictions on powers of States

3. No State shall, without the Consent of Congress, lay any Duty of Tonnage, keep Troops, or Ships of War in time of Peace, enter into any Agreement or Compact with another State, or with a foreign Power, or engage in War, unless actually invaded, or in such imminent Danger as will not admit of delay.

ARTICLE II

SECTION 1

The President; the executive power

1. The executive Power shall be vested in a President of the United States of America. He shall hold his Office during the Term of four Years, and, together with the Vice President, chosen for the same Term, be elected, as follows

Appointment and qualifications of presidential electors

2. Each State shall appoint, in such Manner as the Legislature thereof may direct, a Number of Electors, equal to the whole Number of Senators and Representatives to which the State may be entitled in the Congress: but no Senator or Representative, or Person holding an Office of Trust or Profit under the United States, shall be appointed an Elector.

Original method of electing the President and Vice President *

[The Electors shall meet in their respective States, and vote by Ballot for two Persons, of whom one at least shall not be an Inhabitant of the same State with themselves. And they shall make a List of all the Persons voted for, and of the Number of Votes for each; which List they shall sign and certify, and transmit sealed to the Seat of the Government of the United States, directed to the President of the Senate. The President of the Senate shall, in the Presence of the Senate and House of Representatives, open all the Certificates, and the Votes shall then be counted. The Person having the greatest Number of Votes shall be the President, if such Number be a Majority of the whole Number of Electors appointed; and if there be more than one who have such Majority, and have an equal Number of Votes, then the House of Representatives shall immediately chuse by Ballot one of them for President; and if no Person have a Majority, then from the five highest on the List the said House shall in like Manner chuse the President. But in chusing the President, the Votes shall be taken by States, the Representation from each State having one Vote; A quorum for this Purpose shall consist of a Member or Members from two thirds of the States and a Majority of all the States shall be necessary to a Choice. In every Case, after the Choice of the President, the Person having the greatest Number of Votes of the Electors shall be the Vice President. But if there should remain two or more who have equal Votes, the Senate should chuse from them by Ballot the Vice President.]

Congress may determine time of choosing electors and day for casting their votes

3. The Congress may determine the Time of chusing the Electors, and the Day on which they shall give their Votes; which Day shall be the same throughout the United States.

---

* *This clause has been superseded by the 12th Amendment.*

Qualifications for the office of President †

4. No Person except a natural born Citizen, or a Citizen of the United States, at the time of the Adoption of this Constitution, shall be eligible to the Office of President; neither shall any Person be eligible to that Office who shall not have attained to the Age of thirty five Years, and been fourteen Years a Resident within the United States.

Filling vacancy in the office of President ‡

5. In Case of the Removal of the President from Office, or of his death, Resignation, or Inability to discharge the Powers and Duties of the said Office, the Same shall devolve on the Vice President, and the Congress may by Law provide for the Case of Removal, Death, Resignation or Inability, both of the President and Vice President, declaring what Officer shall then act as President, and such Officer shall act accordingly, until the Disability be removed, or a President shall be elected.

Compensation of the President

6. The President shall, at stated Times, receive for his Services, a Compensation, which shall neither be encreased nor diminished during the Period for which he shall have been elected, and he shall not receive within that Period any other Emolument from the United States, or any of them.

Oath to be taken by the President

7. Before he enter on the Execution of his Office, he shall take the following Oath or Affirmation:—"I do solemnly swear (or affirm) that I will faithfully execute the Office of President of the United States, and will to the best of my Ability, preserve, protect and defend the Constitution of the United States."

SECTION 2

The President to be commander in chief of army and navy and head of executive departments; may grant reprieves and pardons

1. The President shall be Commander in Chief of the Army and Navy of the United States, and of the Militia of the several States, when

---

† For qualifications of the Vice President, see 12th Amendment.
‡ Amended by the 20th Amendment, Sections 3 and 4.

called into the actual Service of the United States; he may require the Opinion, in writing, of the principal Officer in each of the executive Departments, upon any Subject relating to the Duties of their respective Offices, and he shall have Power to grant Reprieves and Pardons for Offences against the United States, except in Cases of Impeachment.

President may, with concurrence of Senate, make treaties, appoint ambassadors, etc.; appointment of inferior officers, authority of Congress over

2. He shall have Power, by and with the Advice and Consent of the Senate, to make Treaties, provided two thirds of the Senators present concur; and he shall nominate, and by and with the Advice and Consent of the Senate, shall appoint Ambassadors, other public Ministers and Consuls, Judges of the supreme Court, and all other Officers of the United States, whose Appointments are not herein otherwise provided for, and which shall be established by Law: but the Congress may by Law vest the Appointment of such inferior Officers, as they think proper, in the President alone, in the Courts of Law, or in the Heads of Departments.

President may fill vacancies in office during recess of Senate

3. The President shall have Power to fill up all Vacancies that may happen during the Recess of the Senate, by granting Commissions which shall expire at the End of their next Session.

SECTION 3

President to give advice to Congress; may convene or adjourn it on certain occasions; to receive ambassadors, etc.; have laws executed and commission all officers

He shall from time to time give to the Congress Information of the State of the Union, and recommend to their Consideration such Measures as he shall judge necessary and expedient; he may, on extraordinary Occasions, convene both Houses or either of them, and in Case of Disagreement between them, with Respect to the Time of Adjournment, he may adjourn them to such Time as he shall think proper; he shall receive Ambassadors and other public Ministers; he shall take Care that the Laws be faithfully executed, and shall Commission all the Officers of the United States.

Section 4

All civil officers removable by impeachment

1. The President, Vice President and all civil Officers of the United States, shall be removed from Office on Impeachment for, and Conviction of, Treason, Bribery, or other high Crimes and Misdemeanors.

ARTICLE III

Section 1

Judicial powers; how vested; term of office and compensation of judges

The judicial Power of the United States, shall be vested in one supreme Court, and in such inferior Courts as the Congress may from time to time ordain and establish. The Judges, both of the supreme and inferior Courts, shall hold their Offices during good Behaviour, and shall, at stated Times, receive for their Services, a Compensation, which shall not be diminished during their Continuance in Office.

Section 2

Jurisdiction of Federal courts*

1. The judicial Power shall extend to all Cases, in Law and Equity, arising under this Constitution, the Laws of the United States, and Treaties made, or which shall be made, under their Authority;— to all Cases affecting Ambassadors, other public Ministers and Consuls; —to all Cases of Admirality and maritime Jurisdiction;—to Controversies to which the United States shall be a Party;—to Controversies between two or more States;—between a State and Citizens of another State;—between Citizens of different States,—between Citizens of the same State claiming Lands under Grants of different States, and between a State, or the Citizens thereof, and foreign States, Citizens or Subjects.

Original and appellate jurisdiction of Supreme Court

2. In all Cases affecting Ambassadors, other public Ministers and Consuls, and those in which a State shall be Party, the supreme Court shall have original Jurisdiction. In all the other Cases before

* This section is abridged by the 11th Amendment.

mentioned, the supreme Court shall have appellate Jurisdiction, both as to Law and Fact, with such Exceptions, and under such Regulations as the Congress shall make.

Trial of all crimes, except impeachment, to be by jury

3. The Trial of all Crimes, except in Cases of Impeachment, shall be by Jury; and such Trial shall be held in the State where the said Crimes shall have been committed, but when not committed within any State, the Trial shall be at such Place or Places as the Congress may by Law have directed.

SECTION 3

Treason defined; conviction of

1. Treason against the United States, shall consist only in levying War against them, or in adhering to their Enemies, giving them Aid and Comfort. No Person shall be convicted of Treason unless on the Testimony of two Witnesses to the same overt Act; or on Confession in open Court.

Congress to declare punishment for treason; proviso

2. The Congress shall have Power to declare the Punishment of Treason, but no Attainder of Treason shall work Corruption of Blood, or Forfeiture except during the Life of the Person attained.

ARTICLE IV

SECTION 1

Each State to give full faith and credit to the public acts and records of other States

Full Faith and Credit shall be given in each State to the public Acts, Records, and judicial Proceedings of every other State. And the Congress may by general Laws prescribe the Manner in which such Acts, Records and Proceedings shall be proved, and the Effect thereof.

SECTION 2

Privileges of citizens

1. The Citizens of each State shall be entitled to all Privileges and Immunities of Citizens in the several States.

Extradition between the several States

2. A Person charged in any State with Treason, Felony, or other Crime, who shall flee from Justice, and be found in another State, shall on Demand of the executive Authority of the State from which he fled, be delivered up, to be removed to the State having Jurisdiction of the Crime.

Persons held to labor or service in one State, fleeing to another, to be returned *

3. No Person held to Service or Labour in one State, under the Laws thereof, escaping into another, shall, in Consequence of any Law or Regulation therein, be discharged from such Service or Labour, but shall be delivered up on Claim of the Party to whom such Service or Labour may be due.

Section 3

New States

1. New States may be admitted by the Congress into this Union; but no new State shall be formed or erected within the Jurisdiction of any other State; nor any State be formed by the Junction of two or more States, or Parts of States, without the Consent of the Legislatures of the States concerned as well as of the Congress.

Regulations concerning territory

2. The Congress shall have Power to dispose of and make all needful Rules and Regulations respecting the Territory or other Property belonging to the United States; and nothing in this Constitution shall be so construed as to Prejudice any Claims of the United States, or of any particular State.

Section 4

Republican form of government and protection guaranteed the several States

The United States shall guarantee to every State in this Union a Republican Form of Government, and shall protect each of them against Invasion; and on Application of the Legislature, or of the Executive (when the Legislature cannot be convened) against domestic Violence.

---

* See the 13th Amendment.

THE CONSTITUTION OF THE UNITED STATES

ARTICLE V

Ways in which the Constitution can be amended

The Congress, whenever two thirds of both Houses shall deem it necessary, shall propose Amendments to this Constitution, or, on the Application of the Legislatures of two thirds of the several States, shall call a Convention for proposing Amendments, which, in either Case, shall be valid to all Intents and Purposes, as Part of this Constitution, when ratified by the Legislatures of three fourths of the several States, or by Conventions in three fourths thereof, as the one or the other Mode of Ratification may be proposed by the Congress; Provided that no Amendment which may be made prior to the Year One thousand eight hundred and eight shall in any Manner affect the first and fourth Clauses in the Ninth Section of the first Article; and that no State, without its Consent, shall be deprived of its equal Suffrage in the Senate.

ARTICLE VI

Debts contracted under the confederation secured

1. All Debts contracted and Engagements entered into, before the Adoption of this Constitution, shall be as valid against the United States under this Constitution, as under the Confederation.

Concerning this immortal instrument of government, James Bryce, Viscount of Dechmont, has said:

The Constitution of the United States, including the amendments, may be read aloud in twenty-three minutes. It is about half as long as Saint Paul's Epistle to the Corinthians and one-fourth as long as the Irish Land Act of 1881. History knows few instruments which in so few words lay down equally momentous rules on a vast range of matters of the highest importance and complexity.

THE CONSTITUTION OF THE UNITED STATES

Constitution, laws and treaties of the United States to be supreme

2. This Constitution, and the Laws of the United States which shall be made in Pursuance thereof; and all Treaties made, or which shall be made, under the Authority of the United States, shall be the supreme Law of the Land; and the Judges in every State shall be bound thereby, any Thing in the Constitution or Laws of any State to the Contrary notwithstanding.

Who shall take constitutional oath; no religious test as to official qualification

3. The Senators and Representatives before mentioned, and the Members of the several State Legislatures, and all executive and judicial Officers, both of the United States and of the several States, shall be bound by Oath or Affirmation, to support this Constitution; but no religious Test shall ever be required as a Qualification to any Office or public Trust under the United States.

ARTICLE VII

Constitution to be considered adopted when ratified by nine States

The Ratification of the Conventions of nine States shall be sufficient for the Establishment of this Constitution between the States so ratifying the Same.

AMENDMENTS TO THE CONSTITUTION OF THE UNITED STATES

Amendments I to X inclusive are popularly known as the
BILL OF RIGHTS.

ARTICLE I

Freedom of religion, speech, of the press, and right of petition

Congress shall make no law respecting an establishment of religion, or prohibiting the free exercise thereof; or abridging the freedom of speech, or of the press; or the right of the people peaceably to assemble, and to petition the Government for a redress of grievances.

ARTICLE II

Right of people to bear arms not to be infringed

A well regulated Militia, being necessary to the security of a free State, the right of the people to keep and bear Arms, shall not be infringed.

ARTICLE III

Quartering of troops

No Soldier shall, in time of peace be quartered in any house, without the consent of the Owner, nor in time of war, but in a manner to be prescribed by law.

ARTICLE IV

Persons and houses to be secure from unreasonable searches and seizures

The right of the people to be secure in their persons, houses, papers, and effects, against unreasonable searches and seizures, shall not be violated, and no Warrants shall issue, but upon probable cause, supported by Oath or affirmation, and particularly describing the place to be searched, and the persons or things to be seized.

ARTICLE V

Trials for crimes; just compensation for private property taken for public use

No person shall be held to answer for a capital, or otherwise infamous crime, unless on a presentment or indictment of a Grand Jury, except in cases arising in the land or naval forces, or in the Militia, when in actual service in time of War or public danger; nor shall any person be subject for the same offence to be twice put in jeopardy of life or limb, nor shall be compelled in any criminal case to be a witness against himself, nor be deprived of life, liberty, or property, without due process of law; nor shall private property be taken for public use, without just compensation.

THE CONSTITUTION OF THE UNITED STATES

ARTICLE VI

Civil rights in trials for crimes enumerated

In all criminal prosecutions, the accused shall enjoy the right to a speedy and public trial, by an impartial jury of the State and district wherein the crime shall have been committed, which district shall have been previously ascertained by law, and to be informed of the nature and cause of the accusation; to be confronted with the witnesses against him; to have compulsory process for obtaining witnesses in his favor, and to have the Assistance of Counsel for his defense.

ARTICLE VII

Civil rights in civil suits

In Suits at common law, where the value in controversy shall exceed twenty dollars, the right of trial by jury shall be preserved, and no fact tried by a jury, shall be otherwise re-examined in any Court of the United States, than according to the rules of the common law.

ARTICLE VIII

Excessive bail, fines and punishments prohibited

Excessive bail shall not be required, nor excessive fines imposed, nor cruel and unusual punishments inflicted.

ARTICLE IX

Reserved rights of people

The enumeration in the Constitution, of certain rights, shall not be construed to deny or disparage others retained by the people.

ARTICLE X

Powers not delegated, reserved to states and people respectively

The powers not delegated to the United States by the Constitution, nor prohibited by it to the States, are reserved to the States respectively, or to the people.

THE CONSTITUTION OF THE UNITED STATES

ARTICLE XI

Judicial power of United States not to extend to suits against a State

The Judicial power of the United States shall not be construed to extend to any suit in law or equity, commenced or prosecuted against one of the United States by Citizens of another State, or by Citizens or Subjects of any Foreign State.

ARTICLE XII

Present mode of electing President and Vice-President by electors *

The Electors shall meet in their respective states and vote by ballot for President and Vice-President, one of whom, at least, shall not be an inhabitant of the same state with themselves; they shall name in their ballots the person voted for as President, and in distinct ballots the person voted for as Vice-President, and they shall make distinct lists of all persons voted for as President, and of all persons voted for as Vice-President, and of the number of votes for each, which lists they shall sign and certify, and transmit sealed to the seat of the government of the United States, directed to the President of the Senate;—The President of the Senate shall, in the presence of the Senate and House of Representatives, open all the certificates and the votes shall then be counted;—The person having the greatest number of votes for President, shall be the President, if such number be a majority of the whole number of Electors appointed; and if no person have such majority, then from the persons having the highest numbers not exceeding three on the list of those voted for as President, the House of Representatives shall choose immediately, by ballot, the President. But in choosing the President, the votes shall be taken by states, the representation from each state having one vote; a quorum for this purpose shall consist of a member or members from two-thirds of the states, and a majority of all the states shall be necessary to a choice. And if the House of Representatives shall not choose a President whenever the right of choice shall devolve upon them, before the fourth day of March next following, then the Vice-President shall act as President, as in the case of the death or other constitutional disability of the President.—The person having the greatest number of votes as Vice-President, shall be the Vice-President, if such number be a majority of the whole number

---

* *Amended by the 20th Amendment, Sections 3 and 4.*

37

THE CONSTITUTION OF THE UNITED STATES

of Electors appointed, and if no person have a majority, then from the two highest numbers on the list, the Senate shall choose the Vice-President; a quorum for the purpose shall consist of two-thirds of the whole number of Senators, and a majority of the whole number shall be necessary to a choice. But no person constitutionally ineligible to the office of President shall be eligible to that of Vice-President of the United States.

ARTICLE XIII

SECTION 1

Slavery prohibited

Neither slavery nor involuntary servitude, except as a punishment for crime whereof the party shall have been duly convicted, shall exist within the United States, or any place subject to their jurisdiction.

SECTION 2

Congress given power to enforce this article

Congress shall have power to enforce this article by appropriate legislation.

ARTICLE XIV

SECTION 1

Citizenship defined; privileges of citizens

All persons born or naturalized in the United States, and subject to the jurisdiction thereof, are citizens of the United States and of the State wherein they reside. No State shall make or enforce any law which shall abridge the privileges or immunities of citizens of the United States; nor shall any State deprive any person of life, liberty, or property, without due process of law; nor deny to any person within its jurisdiction the equal protection of the laws.

SECTION 2

Apportionment of Representatives

Representatives shall be apportioned among the several States according to their respective numbers, counting the whole number of persons in each State, excluding Indians not taxed. But when the right to vote at any election for the choice of electors for President and Vice-President of the United States, Representatives in Congress, the Executive and Judicial officers of a State, or the members of the Legislature thereof, is denied to any of the male inhabitants of such State, being twenty-one years of age, and citizens of the United States, or in any way abridged, except for participation in rebellion, or other crime, the basis of representation therein shall be reduced in the proportion which the number of such male citizens shall bear to the whole number of male citizens twenty-one years of age in such State.

SECTION 3

Disqualification for office; removal of disability

No person shall be a Senator or Representative in Congress, or elector of President and Vice President, or hold any office, civil or military, under the United States, or under any State, who, having previously taken an oath, as a member of Congress, or as an officer of the United States, or as a member of any State legislature, or as an executive or judicial officer of any State, to support the Constitution of the United States, shall have engaged in insurrection or rebellion against the same, or given aid or comfort to the enemies thereof. But Congress may by a vote of two-thirds of each House, remove such disability.

SECTION 4

Public debt not to be questioned; payment of debts and claims incurred in aid of rebellion forbidden

The validity of the public debt of the United States, authorized by law, including debts incurred for payment of pensions and bounties for services in suppressing insurrection or rebellion, shall not be questioned. But neither the United States nor any State shall assume or pay any debt or obligation incurred in aid of insurrection or rebellion against the United States, or any claim for the loss or emancipation of any slave; but all such debts, obligations and claims shall be held illegal and void.

SECTION 5

Congress given power to enforce this article

The Congress shall have power to enforce, by appropriate legislation, the provisions of this article.

THE CONSTITUTION OF THE UNITED STATES
ARTICLE XV
SECTION 1
Right of certain citizens to vote established

The right of citizens of the United States to vote shall not be denied or abridged by the United States or by any State on account of race, color, or previous condition of servitude.

SECTION 2
Congress given power to enforce this article

The Congress shall have power to enforce this article by appropriate legislation.

ARTICLE XVI
Taxes on income; Congress given power to lay and collect

The Congress shall have power to lay and collect taxes on incomes, from whatever source derived, without apportionment among the several states, and without regard to any census or enumeration.

ARTICLE XVII
Election of United States Senators; filling of vacancies; qualifications of electors

1. The Senate of the United States shall be composed of two Senators from each State, elected by the people thereof, for six years; and each Senator shall have one vote. The electors in each State shall have the qualifications requisite for electors of the most numerous branch of the State legislatures.

2. When vacancies happen in the representation of any State in the Senate, the executive authority of such State shall issue writs of election to fill such vacancies: *Provided,* That the legislature of any State may empower the executive thereof to make temporary appointment until the people fill the vacancies by election as the legislature may direct.

3. This amendment shall not be so construed as to affect the election or term of any Senator chosen before it becomes valid as part of the Constitution.

THE CONSTITUTION OF THE UNITED STATES
ARTICLE XVIII *

Manufacture, sale or transportation of intoxicating liquors, for beverage purposes, prohibited

1. After one year from the ratification of this article the manufacture, sale, or transportation of intoxicating liquors within, the importation thereof into, or the exportation thereof from the United States and all territory subject to the jurisdiction thereof for beverage purposes is hereby prohibited.

Congress and the several States given concurrent power to pass appropriate legislation to enforce this article

2. The Congress and the several States shall have concurrent power to enforce this article by appropriate legislation.

Provision of article to become operative, when adopted by three-fourths of the States

3. This article shall be inoperative unless it shall have been ratified as an amendment to the Constitution by the legislatures of the several States, as provided in the Constitution, within seven years from the date of the submission hereof to the States by the Congress.

ARTICLE XIX

The right of citizens to vote shall not be denied because of sex

The right of citizens of the United States to vote shall not be denied or abridged by the United States or by any States on account of sex.

Congress shall have power to enforce this article by appropriate legislation.

ARTICLE XX

SECTION 1

Terms of President, Vice-President, Senators and Representatives

The terms of the President and Vice-President shall end at noon on the twentieth day of January, and the terms of Senators and Representatives at noon on the third day of January, of the years in

---

* *Repealed by the 21st Amendment.*

which such terms would have ended if this article had not been ratified; and the terms of their successors shall then begin.

SECTION 2

Time of assembling Congress

The Congress shall assemble at least once in every year, and such meeting shall begin at noon on the third day of January, unless they shall by law appoint a different day.

SECTION 3

Filling vacancies in office of President

If, at the time fixed for the beginning of the term of the President, the President-elect shall have died, the Vice-President-elect shall become President. If a President shall not have been chosen before the time fixed for the beginning of his term, or if the President-elect shall have failed to qualify, then the Vice-President-elect shall act as President until a President shall have qualified; and the Congress may by law provide for the case wherein neither a President-elect nor a Vice-President-elect shall have qualified, declaring who shall then act as President, or the manner in which one who is to act shall be selected, and such person shall act accordingly until a President or Vice-President shall have qualified.

SECTION 4

Power of Congress in Presidential succession

The Congress may by law provide for the case of the death of any of the persons from whom the House of Representatives may choose a President whenever the right of choice shall have devolved upon them, and for the case of the death of any of the persons from whom the Senate may choose a Vice-President whenever the right of choice shall have devolved upon them.

SECTION 5

Time of taking effect

Sections 1 and 2 shall take effect on the 15th day of October following the ratification of this article.

THE CONSTITUTION OF THE UNITED STATES

SECTION 6

Ratification

This article shall be inoperative unless it shall have been ratified as an amendment to the Constitution by the legislatures of three-fourths of the several States within seven years from the date of its submission.

ARTICLE XXI

SECTION 1

Repeal of Prohibition Amendment

The eighteenth article of amendment to the Constitution of the United States is hereby repealed.

SECTION 2

Transportation of intoxicating liquors

The transportation or importation into any State, Territory, or possession of the United States for delivery or use therein of intoxicating liquors, in violation of the laws thereof, is hereby prohibited.

SECTION 3

Ratification

This article shall be inoperative unless it shall have been ratified as an amendment to the Constitution by conventions in the several States, as provided in the Constitution, within seven years from the date of the submission hereof to the States by the Congress.

ARTICLE XXII

SECTION 1

Limit to number of terms a President may serve

No person shall be elected to the office of the President more than twice, and no person who has held the office of President, or acted as President, for more than two years of a term to which some other person was elected President shall be elected to the office of the President more than once. But this Article shall not apply to any

THE CONSTITUTION OF THE UNITED STATES

person holding the office of President when this Article was proposed by the Congress, and shall not prevent any person who may be holding the office of President, or acting as President, during the term within which this Article becomes operative from holding the office of President or acting as President during the remainder of such term.

SECTION 2

Ratification

This article shall be inoperative unless it shall have been ratified as an amendment to the Constitution by the legislatures of three-fourths of the several States within seven years from the date of its submission to the States by the Congress.

ARTICLE XXIII

SECTION 1

Electors for the District of Columbia

The District constituting the seat of Government of the United States shall appoint in such manner as the Congress may direct:

A number of electors of President and Vice President equal to the whole number of Senators and Representatives in Congress to which the District would be entitled if it were a State, but in no event more than the least populous State; they shall be in addition to those appointed by the States, but they shall be considered, for the purposes of the election of President and Vice President, to be electors appointed by a State; and they shall meet in the District and perform such duties as provided by the twelfth article of amendment.

SECTION 2

Enforcement

The Congress shall have the power to enforce this article by appropriate legislation.

ARTICLE XXIV

SECTION 1

Citizens' Right to Vote in Federal Elections

The right of citizens of the United States to vote in any primary or other election for President or Vice President, for electors for

President or Vice President, or for Senator or Representative in Congress, shall not be denied or abridged by the United States or any State by reason of failure to pay any poll tax or other tax.

SECTION 2

The Congress shall have power to enforce this article by appropriate legislation.

ARTICLE XXV

SECTION 1

Filling the Offices of President or Vice President in Case of Vacancy

In case of the removal of the President from office or of his death or resignation, the Vice President shall become President.

SECTION 2

Whenever there is a vacancy in the office of the Vice President, the President shall nominate a Vice President who shall take office upon confirmation by a majority vote of both Houses of Congress.

SECTION 3

Whenever the President transmits to the President pro tempore of the Senate and the Speaker of the House of Representatives his written declaration that he is unable to discharge the powers and duties of his office, and until he transmits to them a written declaration to the contrary, such powers and duties shall be discharged by the Vice President as Acting President.

SECTION 4

Whenever the Vice President and a majority of either the principal officers of the executive departments or of such other body as Congress may by law provide, transmit to the President pro tempore of the Senate and the Speaker of the House of Representatives their written declaration that the President is unable to discharge the powers and duties of his office, the Vice President shall immediately assume the powers and duties of the office as Acting President.

Thereafter, when the President transmits to the President pro tempore of the Senate and the Speaker of the House of Representatives his written declaration that no inability exists, he shall resume the powers and duties of his office unless the Vice President and a majority of either the principal officers of the executive department or of such other body as Congress may by law provide, transmit within four days to the President pro tempore of the Senate and the Speaker of the House of Representatives their written declaration that the President is unable to discharge the powers and duties of his office. Thereupon Congress shall decide the issue, assembling within forty-eight hours for that purpose if not in session. If the Congress, within twenty-one days after the receipt of the latter written declaration, or, if Congress is not in session, within twenty-one days after Congress is required to assemble, determines by two-thirds vote of both Houses that the President is unable to discharge the powers and duties of his office, the Vice President shall continue to discharge the same as Acting President; otherwise, the President shall resume the powers and duties of his office.

ARTICLE XXVI
SECTION 1
Citizens eighteen years of age right to vote

The right of citizens of the United States, who are eighteen years of age or older, to vote shall not be denied or abridged by the United States or by any State on account of age.

SECTION 2

The Congress shall have power to enforce this article by appropriate legislation.

RATIFICATION OF THE CONSTITUTION

The proposed Constitution was approved by the Convention on September 17, 1787, and was subsequently ratified by the several States, on the following dates: Delaware, December 7, 1787; Pennsylvania, December 12, 1787; New Jersey, December 18, 1787; Georgia, January 2, 1788; Connecticut, January 9, 1788; Massachusetts, February 6, 1788; Maryland, April 28, 1788; South Carolina, May 23, 1788; New Hampshire, June 21, 1788; Virginia, June 26, 1788; New York, July 26, 1788; North Carolina, November 21, 1789; Rhode Island, May 29, 1790.

(Ratification was effective when ratified by the ninth State— New Hampshire)

RELATING TO THE CONSTITUTION

O N June 28, 1787, when the Constitutional Convention found itself in great confusion and could not agree upon a course of action, the serene Benjamin Franklin arose in his place and addressed the President, George Washington:

"We have been assured, Sir, in the Sacred Writings, that— 'Except the Lord Build the House, they labor in vain that build it.' I firmly believe this; and I also believe that without His concurring aid, we shall succeed in this political building no better than the builders of Babel; we shall be divided in our little partial local interests, our projects will be confounded and we ourselves shall become a reproach and a bye word down to future ages. And what is worse, mankind may hereafter, from this unfortunate instance, despair of establishing Government by human wisdom and leave it to chance, war or conquest. I therefore beg leave to move—

"That henceforth, Prayers imploring the assistance of Heaven, and its blessings on our deliberations, be held in this Assembly every morning before we proceed to business, and that one or more of the clergy of this city be requested to officiate in that service."

The chairman of the convention that framed our Constitution was George Washington. On the back of his chair there was a painting of the sun as it appeared just above the horizon. When, after many months of wrangling and discussions which often threatened to break up the convention entirely, the Constitution was finally signed by the 39 delegates, Benjamin Franklin, then 83 years old, who had been a great stabilizing force in the convention, arose and said: "I have looked at that painting again and again. I have wondered whether it was a rising or a setting sun, but now I know it is a rising sun."

Now we must see to it that this sun that has shone upon us with such favor, that has seen America grow from a weak little group of colonies into the greatest of all nations, does not set.

RELATING TO THE CONSTITUTION

Writing the Constitution was a new task for men. And when they had finished it they described it as *"Novus ordo seclorum"*—the new order of the ages—as you will find engraved on your dollar bills, a quotation of Virgil nearly 2,000 years before. They wrought better than they knew, as all men know. For they had at last produced a balanced structure of power in which equality, justice, and liberty were in equilibrium.

The significant fact is that the American colonists fought and died to establish and preserve the principle of human freedom against what was then one of the greatest powers in the world. There were voices then, which told them they were weak, unprepared, not strong enough nor brave enough to challenge the power of the British Empire. These were the voices which counseled the ancient version of modern-day "peaceful co-existence." But the Founding Fathers did not listen. They knew for what they stood and were willing, if need be, to fight for it. It is well to remember that the cannonballs which exploded on Bunker Hill looked just as formidable and equally as destructive to our ancestors as a nuclear bomb does to us. But they knew that a principle is not successfully defended by the timid and the appeaser. And so they bequeathed to us a republic and a system that made us great, powerful and free. On that first American Independence Day a band of brave men "pledged their lives, their fortunes and their sacred honor" to the battle for human freedom. Can we do less?

With malice toward none, with charity for all, with firmness in the right as God gives us to see the right, let us strive on to finish the work we are in, to bind up the nation's wounds, to care for him who shall have borne the battle and for his widow and orphans, to do all which may achieve and cherish a just and a lasting peace among ourselves and with all nations.

—*Abraham Lincoln*

THE PRESIDENTS
OF THE UNITED STATES
OF AMERICA

Portraits of Presidents reproduced by permission of and copyright by Brown & Bigelow, a Division of Standard Packaging Corporation, St. Paul, Minn.

GEORGE WASHINGTON
1st President 1789-1797

JOHN ADAMS
2nd President 1797-1801

THOMAS JEFFERSON
3rd President 1801-1809

JAMES MADISON
4th President 1809-1817

JAMES MONROE
5th President 1817-1825

JOHN QUINCY ADAMS
6th President 1825-1829

ANDREW JACKSON
7th President 1829-1837

MARTIN VAN BUREN
8th President 1837-1841

WM. HENRY HARRISON
9th President 1841

JOHN TYLER
10th President 1841-1845

JAMES KNOX POLK
11th President 1845-1849

ZACHARY TAYLOR
12th President 1849-1850

MILLARD FILLMORE
13th President 1850-1853

FRANKLIN PIERCE
14th President 1853-1857

JAMES BUCHANAN
15th President 1857-1861

ABRAHAM LINCOLN
16th President 1861-1865

ANDREW JOHNSON
17th President 1865-1869

ULYSSES S. GRANT
18th President 1869-1877

RUTHERFORD B. HAYES
19th President 1877-1881

JAMES A. GARFIELD
20th President 1881

CHESTER A. ARTHUR
21st President 1881-1885

GROVER CLEVELAND
22nd President 1885-1889
24th President 1893-1897

BENJAMIN HARRISON
23rd President 1889-1893

WILLIAM McKINLEY
25th President 1897-1901

51

THEODORE ROOSEVELT
26th President 1901-1909

WM. HOWARD TAFT
27th President 1909-1913

WOODROW WILSON
28th President 1913-1921

WARREN G. HARDING
29th President 1921-1923

CALVIN COOLIDGE
30th President 1923-1929

HERBERT HOOVER
31st President 1929-1933

FRANKLIN ROOSEVELT
32nd President 1933-1945

HARRY S. TRUMAN
33rd President 1945-1953

DWIGHT D. EISENHOWER
34th President 1953-1961

JOHN F. KENNEDY
35th President 1961-1963

LYNDON B. JOHNSON
36th President 1963-1969

RICHARD M. NIXON
37th President 1969-1974

GERALD FORD
38th President 1974-1977

JAMES EARL CARTER
39th President 1977-1981

RONALD REAGAN
40th President 1981-

Let it be remembered that civil liberty consists not in a right to every man to do just what he pleases; but it consists in an equal right to all the citizens to have, enjoy, and do, in peace, security, and without molestation, whatever the equal and constitutional laws of the country admit to be consistent with the public good.

—John Jay, 1790

We speak of Liberty as one thing, and of virtue, wealth, knowledge, invention, national strength and national independence as other things. But, of all these, Liberty is the source, the mother, the necessary condition. She is to virtue what light is to color; to wealth what sunshine is to grain; to knowledge what eyes are to sight. She is the genius of invention, the brawn of national strength, the spirit of national independence. Where Liberty rises, there virtue grows, wealth increases, knowledge expands, invention multiplies human powers, and in strength and spirit the freer nation rises among her neighbors...

—Henry George, 1879

EXCERPTS FROM
THE FEDERALIST, NO. 10

NOVEMBER 23, 1787

JAMES MADISON

THERE are two methods of curing the mischiefs of faction: the one, by removing its causes; the other by controlling its effects. . . .

The diversity in the faculties of men, from which the rights of property originate, is not less an insuperable obstacle to a uniformity of interests. The protection of these faculties is the first object of government. From the protection of different and unequal faculties of acquiring property, the possession of different degrees and kinds of property immediately results; and from the influence of these on the sentiments and views of the respective proprietors, ensues a division of the society into different interests and parties. . . .

But the most common and durable source of factions has been the various and unequal distribution of property. Those who hold and those who are without property have ever formed distinct interests in society. . . .

The inference to which we are brought is, that the *causes* of faction cannot be removed, and that relief is only to be sought in the means of controlling its *effects.*

If a faction consists of less than a majority, relief is supplied by the republican principle, which enables the majority to defeat its sinister views by regular vote. It may clog the administration, it may convulse the society; but it will be unable to execute and mask its violence under the forms of the Constitution. . . .

JAMES MADISON
1751 - 1836

EXCERPTS FROM WASHINGTON'S FAREWELL ADDRESS .

UNITED STATES, SEPTEMBER 19, 1796
AFTER ANNOUNCING HIS RETIREMENT FROM PUBLIC LIFE,
PRESIDENT GEORGE WASHINGTON SAID:

. . . . Here, perhaps, I ought to stop. But a solicitude for your welfare . . . and the apprehension of danger, natural to that solicitude, urge me . . . to offer to your solemn contemplation, and to recommend to your frequent review, some sentiments; which are the result of much reflection, of no inconsiderable observation, and which appear to me all important to the permanency of your felicity as a People. These will be offered to you . . . as . . . the disinterested warnings of a parting friend, who can possibly have no personal motive to bias his counsel. . . .

Interwoven as is the love of liberty with every ligament of your hearts, no recommendation of mine is necessary to fortify or confirm the attachment.

The Unity of Government which constitutes you one people is also now dear to you. It is justly so; for it is a main Pillar in the Edifice of your real independence, the support of your tranquility at home; your peace abroad; of your safety; of your prosperity; of that very Liberty which you so highly prize. But as it is easy to foresee, that from different causes and from different quarters, much pains will be taken, many artifices employed, to weaken in your minds the conviction of this truth; as this is the point in your political fortress against which the batteries of internal and external enemies will be most constantly and actively (though often covertly and insidiously) directed, it is of infinite moment, that you should properly estimate the immense value of your national Union to your collective and individual happiness; that you should cherish a cordial, habitual and immoveable attachment to it; accustoming yourself to think and speak of it as of the Palladium of your political safety and prosperity; watching for its preservation with jealous anxiety; discountenancing whatever may suggest even a suspicion that it can in any event be abandoned, and indignantly frowning upon the first dawning of every attempt to alienate any portion of our Country from the rest, or to enfeeble the sacred ties which now link together the various parts.

For this you have every inducement of sympathy and interest. Citizens by birth or choice, of a common country, that country has a right to concentrate your affections. The name of AMERICAN, which belongs to you . . . must always exalt the just pride of Patriotism, more than any appellation derived from local discriminations. With slight shades of difference, you have the same Religion, Manners, Habits and political Principles. You have in a common cause fought and triumphed together. The independence and liberty you possess are the work of joint councils, and joint efforts; of common dangers, sufferings and successes. . . .

In contemplating the causes wch. may disturb our Union, it occurs as matter of serious concern, that any ground should have been furnished for characterizing parties by *Geographical* discriminations: *Northern* and *Southern; Atlantic* and *Western;* whence designing men may endeavour to excite a belief that there is a real difference of local interests and views. One of the expedients of Party to acquire influence, within particular districts, is to misrepresent the opinions and aims of other Districts. You cannot shield yourselves too much against the jealousies and heart burnings which spring from these misrepresentations. They tend to render alien to each other those who ought to be bound together by fraternal affection. . . .

To the efficacy and permanency of Your Union, a Government for the whole is indispensable. . . . Sensible of this momentous truth, you have improved upon your first essay, by the adoption of a Constitution of Government, better calculated than your former for an intimate Union, and for the efficacious management of your common concerns. This government, the offspring of our own choice uninfluenced and unawed, adopted upon full investigation and mature deliberation, completely free in its principles, in the distribution of its powers, uniting security with energy, and containing within itself a provision for its own amendment, has a just claim to your confidence and your support. Respect for its authority, compliance with its Laws, acquiescence in its measures, are duties enjoined by the fundamental maxims of true Liberty. The basis of our political systems is the right of the people to make and to alter their Constitutions of Government. But the Constitution which at any time exists, 'till changed by an explicit and authentic act of the whole People, is sacredly obligatory upon all. The very idea of the power and the right of the People to establish

FROM WASHINGTON'S FAREWELL ADDRESS

Government presupposes the duty of every Individual to obey the established Government.

All obstructions to the execution of the Laws, all combinations and Associations, under whatever plausible character, with the real design to direct, controul, counteract, or awe the regular deliberation and action of the constituted authorities are destructive of this fundamental principle and of fatal tendency. They serve to organize faction, to give it an artificial and extraordinary force; to put in the place of the delegated will of the Nation, the will of a party; often a small but artful and enterprizing minority of the community; and, according to the alternate triumphs of different parties, to make the public administration the mirror of the ill concerted and incongruous projects of faction, rather than the Organ of consistent and wholesome plans digested by common councils and modefied by mutual interests. However combinations or associations of the above description may now and then answer popular ends, they are likely, in the course of time and things, to become potent engines, by which cunning, ambitious and unprincipled men will be enabled to subvert the Power of the People, and to usurp for themselves the reins of Government; destroying afterwards the very engines which have lifted them to unjust dominion.

Towards the preservation of your Government and the permanency of your present happy state, it is requisite, not only that you steadily discountenance irregular oppositions to its acknowledged authority, but also that you resist with care the spirit of innovation upon its principles however specious the pretexts. One method of assault may be to effect, in the forms of the Constitution, alterations which will impair the energy of the system, and thus to undermine what cannot be directly overthrown. In all the changes to which you may be invited, remember that time and habit are at least as necessary to fix the true character of Governments, as of other human institutions; that experience is the surest standard, by which to test the real tendency of the existing Constitution of a country; that facility in changes upon the credit of mere hypotheses and opinion exposes to perpetual change, from the endless variety of hypotheses and opinion: and remember, especially, that for the efficient management of your common interests, in a country so extensive as ours, a Government of as much vigour as is consistent with the perfect security of Liberty is indispensable. Liberty itself will find in such a Government, with powers properly distributed and adjusted, its surest Guardian. It is indeed little else than a name, where the Government is too feeble to withstand the enterprises of faction, to confine each member of the Society within the limits prescribed by the laws and to maintain all in the secure and tranquil enjoyment of the rights of person and property. . . .

Let me now take a more comprehensive view, and warn you in the most solemn manner against the baneful effects of the Spirit of Party, generally.

This Spirit, unfortunately, is inseperable from our nature, having its root in the strongest passions of the human mind. It exists under different shapes in all Governments, more or less stifled, controuled, or repressed; but in those of the popular form it is seen in its greatest rankness and is truly their worst enemy.

The alternate dominion of one faction over another, sharpened by the spirit of revenge natural to party dissention, which in different ages and countries has perpetrated the most horrid enormities, is itself a frightful despotism. But this leads at length to a more formal and permanent despotism. The disorders and miseries, which result, gradually incline the minds of men to seek security and repose in the absolute power of an Individual: and sooner or later the chief of some prevailing faction more able or more fortunate than his competitors, turns this disposition to the purposes of his own elevation, on the ruins of Public Liberty. . . .

The common and continual mischiefs of the spirit of Party are sufficient to make it the interest and the duty of a wise People to discourage and restrain it.

It is important, likewise, that the habits of thinking in a free Country should inspire caution in those entrusted with its administration, to confine themselves within their respective Constitutional spheres; avoiding in the exercise of the Powers of one department to encroach upon another. The spirit of encroachment tends to consolidate the powers of all the departments in one, and thus to create whatever the form of government, a real despotism. A just estimate of that love of power, and proneness to abuse it, which predominates in the human heart is sufficient to satisfy us of the truth of this position. The necessity of reciprocal checks in the exercise of political power; by dividing and distributing it into different depositories, and constituting each the Guardian of the Public Weal against invasions by the others, has been evinced by experiments ancient and modern; some of them in our country and under our own eyes. To preserve them must be as necessary as to institute them. If in the opinion of the People, the distribution or modification of the Constitutional powers be in any particular wrong, let it be corrected by an amendment in the way which the Constitution designates. But let there be no change by usurpation; for though this, in one instance, may be the instrument of good, it is the customary weapon by which free governments are destroyed. The precedent must always greatly overbalance in permanent evil any partial or transient benefit which the use can at any time yield.

Of all the dispositions and habits which lead to political prosperity, Religion and morality are indispensable supports. In vain would that man claim the tribute of Patriotism, who should labour to subvert these great Pillars of human happiness, these firmest props of the duties of Men and citizens. . . . Let it simply be asked where is the security for property, for reputation, for life, if the sense of religious obligation *desert* the oaths, which are the instruments of investigation in Courts of Justice? And let us with caution indulge the supposition, that morality can be maintained without religion. Whatever may be conceded to the influence of refined education on minds of peculiar structure, reason and experience both forbid us to expect that National morality can prevail in exclusion of religious principle.

'Tis substantially true, that virtue or morality is a necessary spring of popular government. . . . Who that is a sincere friend to it, can look with indifference upon attempts to shake the foundation of the fabric?

Promote then as an object of primary importance, Institutions for the general diffusion of knowledge. In proportion as the structure of a government gives force to public opinion, it is essential that public opinion should be enlightened.

As a very important source of strength and security, cherish public credit. One method of preserving it is to use it as sparingly as possible: avoiding occasions of expence by cultivating peace, but remembering also that timely disbursements to prepare for danger frequently prevent much greater disbursements to repel it; avoiding likewise the accumulation of debt, not only by shunning occasions of expence, but by vigorous exertions in time of Peace to discharge the Debts which unavoidable wars may have occasioned, not ungenerously throwing upon posterity the burthen which we ourselves ought to bear. The execution of these maxims belongs to your Representatives, but it is necessary that public opinion should cooperate. To facilitate to them the performance of their duty, it is essential that you should practically bear in mind, that towards the payment of debts there must be Revenue; that to have Revenue there must be taxes; that no taxes can be devised which are not more or less inconvenient and unpleasant; that the intrinsic embarrassment inseperable from the selection of the proper objects (which is always a choice of difficulties) ought to be a decisive motive for a candid construction of the conduct of the Government in making it, and for a spirit of acquiescence in the measures for obtaining Revenue which the public exigencies may at any time dictate.

Observe good faith and justice towards all Nations. Cultivate peace and harmony with all. Religion and morality enjoin this conduct; and can it be that good policy does not equally enjoin it? It will be worthy of a free, enlightened, and, at no distant period, a great Nation, to give to mankind the magnanimous and too novel example of a People always guided by an exalted justice and benevolence. Who can doubt that in the course of time and things the fruits of such a plan would richly repay any temporary advantages which might be lost by a steady adherence to it? Can it be, that Providence has not connected the permanent felicity of a Nation with its virtue? . . .

Against the insidious wiles of foreign influence, (I conjure you to believe me fellow citizens) the jealousy of a free people ought to be *constantly* awake; since history and experience prove that foreign influence is one of the most baneful foes of Republican Government. But that jealousy to be useful must be impartial; else it becomes the instrument of the very influence to be avoided, instead of a defence against it. Excessive partiality for one foreign nation and excessive dislike of another, cause those whom they actuate to see danger only on one side, and serve to veil and even second the arts of influence on the other. Real Patriots, who may resist the intriegues of the favourite, are liable to become suspected and odious; while its tools and dupes usurp the applause and confidence of the people, to surrender their interests.

The Great rule of conduct for us, in regard to foreign Nations is in extending our commercial relations to have with them as little *political* connection as possible. So far as we have already formed engagements let them be fulfilled, with perfect good faith. Here let us stop.

FROM WASHINGTON'S FAREWELL ADDRESS

Europe has a set of primary interests, which to us have none, or a very remote relation. . . . Hence therefore it must be unwise in us to implicate ourselves, by artificial ties, in the ordinary vicissitudes of her politics, or the ordinary combinations and collisions of her friendships, or enmities: . . .

'Tis our true policy to steer clear of permanent alliances, with any portion of the foreign world—so far, I mean, as we are now at liberty to do it, for let me not be understood as capable of patronising infidility to existing engagements (I hold the maxim no less applicable to public than to private affairs that honesty is always the best policy). . . .

Taking care always to keep ourselves, by suitable establishments, on a respectably defensive posture, we may safely trust to temporary alliances for extraordinary emergencies.

Harmony, liberal intercourse with all Nations, are recommended by policy, humanity and interest. But even our commercial policy should hold an equal and impartial hand: neither seeking nor granting exclusive favours or preferences; consulting the natural course of things; diffusing and diversifying by gentle means the streams of commerce, but forcing nothing; establishing with Powers so disposed—in order to give to trade a stable course, to define the rights of our Merchants, and to enable the Government to support them—conventional rules of intercourse; the best that present circumstances and mutual opinion will permit, but temporary, and liable to be from time to time abandoned or varied, as experience and circumstances shall dictate; constantly keeping in view, that 'tis folly in one Nation to look for disinterested favors from another; that it must pay with a portion of its Independence for whatever it may accept under that character; that by such acceptance, it may place itself in the condition of having given equivalents for nominal favours and yet of being reproached with ingratitude for not giving more. There can be no greater error than to expect, or calculate upon real favours from Nation to Nation. . . .

In offering to you, my Countrymen, these counsels of an old and affectionate friend, I dare not hope they will make the strong and lasting impression, I could wish. . . . But if . . . they may now and then recur to moderate the fury of party spirit, to warn against the mischiefs of foreign Intriegue, to guard against the Impostures of pretended patriotism; this hope will be a full recompence for the solicitude for your welfare, by which they have been dictated. . . .

ADDRESS AT THE DEDICATION OF THE GETTYSBURG NATIONAL CEMETERY

— ABRAHAM LINCOLN
NOVEMBER 19, 1863

Fourscore and seven years ago our fathers brought forth on this continent a new nation, conceived in liberty, and dedicated to the proposition that all men are created equal.

Now we are engaged in a great civil war, testing whether that nation, or any nation so conceived and so dedicated, can long endure. We are met on a great battlefield of that war. We have come to dedicate a portion of that field as a final resting-place for those who here gave their lives that that nation might live. It is altogether fitting and proper that we should do this.

But, in a larger sense, we cannot dedicate—we cannot consecrate—we cannot hallow—this ground. The brave men, living and dead, who struggled here, have consecrated it far above our poor power to add or detract. The world will little note nor long remember what we say here, but it can never forget what they did here. It is for us, the living, rather, to be dedicated here to the unfinished work which they who fought here have thus far so nobly advanced. It is rather for us to be here dedicated to the great task remaining before us—that from these honored dead we take increased devotion to that cause for which they gave the last full measure of devotion; that we here highly resolve that these dead shall not have died in vain; that this nation, under God, shall have a new birth of freedom; and that government of the people, by the people, for the people, shall not perish from the earth.

THE AMERICAN'S CREED

I BELIEVE in the United States of America as a Government of the people, by the people, for the people; whose just powers are derived from the consent of the governed; a democracy in a republic; a sovereign nation of many sovereign states; a perfect union, one and inseparable; established upon those principles of freedom, equality, justice, and humanity for which American patriots sacrificed their lives and fortunes.

I therefore believe it is my duty to my country to love it; to support its Constitution; to obey its laws; to respect its flag; and to defend it against all enemies.

William Tyler Page

GENERAL WASHINGTON AT PRAYER

FREE ENTERPRISE—AN AMERICAN BREAKTHROUGH

BY

CLARENCE B. CARSON

Edited by

WILLIAM G. SIZEMORE, 33°
(Rear Admiral, U.S.N., Ret.)

THE SUPREME COUNCIL, 33°
Ancient and Accepted Scottish Rite of Freemasonry
Mother Jurisdiction, U.S.A.
1733 16th Street, NW, Washington, DC 20009

The American
Accomplishment

THE story of America is, in large, a success story. The country that
sprang from the small English settlement at Jamestown in 1607 has
been a success beyond the possible dreams of those settlers.

Indeed, the productivity of America had become one of the wonders
of the world by the 20th century. For the first hundred or so years after
the first English settlements, great efforts were put into drawing people
to America. But eventually more and more people were drawn to these
shores for reasons of their own. America became for many of the peoples
of the world the land of freedom and opportunity.

As America's material success has mounted, American historians have
often offered a material explanation. America's material achievement, they
say, can be attributed mainly to the abundant natural resources in the land
that became the United States.

This is a strange explanation. It would hardly account for the course
of settlement in the 15th and 16th centuries after the discovery of America.
The Spanish explorers and settlers had concentrated their attention on Central America, the southernmost portions of North America, and northern
South America. The Portuguese focused upon Brazil with their settlements.
The Atlantic Coast to which the English eventually came was virtually ig-
nored by all nations. The French did push southward in the Mississippi
Valley from Canada, but they were generally more interested in the fur
trade than colonizing.

As for natural resources accounting for the success of English America,
the Indians in the regions first settled by the English gave no early indication that this would be the case. The Indians had hardly prospered. Those
along the eastern coast of North America were among the poorest and
most backward of the Indians in the Americas. Nor were the Indians
located in the central plains noticeably better off.

Nor does the natural resource explanation fare any better at the level
of a theory. Many of the materials and natural phenomena we now think
of as natural resources were once either obstacles or useless. The forests
which covered eastern North America were largely obstacles to be cut down
by the Englishmen who sought to farm the region. Swift streams are
obstacles to get across, especially in times of heavy rains and floods. They
only become resources when dams have been built and the backed up waters
are channeled over waterwheels to turn machinery. The minerals that lay

beneath the surface were of little use to the Indians, who had no knowledge of how to make them into objects of use.

Materials become resources when men find uses for them. They become sources of wealth only when they have been developed. In sum, the wealth of America did not spring from something we now call natural resources. They became natural resources when they were developed and put to use.

The main sources of the material achievements of Americans were not material. They were spiritual in character. They arose from the will or spirit to produce. For convenience, they can be thought of as the three I's—incentives, industry, and ingenuity. Of course, men use materials to produce concrete objects, but underlying the concrete production is the spirit and will to produce.

There are many incentives to produce. Men produce to provide for their needs and wants, for food as sustenance, for building to provide shelter and comfort, for clothing for warmth and adornment, and for a great variety of articles for use and pleasure. Men may produce out of a constructive bent, a bent which may be fortified by religion and social teachings, or because such constructive effort is somehow fulfilling and an inward necessity. But central to the will to work is the possibility of keeping what one has produced for his own use or to dispose of as he may will. It is the extent to which people may do this that distinguishes one society from another. Men may be induced to produce when they can keep but a small portion of that which they produce for themselves. But the greatest inducement to production is when men can keep all or most of what they produce for themselves, to dispose of as they will. The extent to which they can do so is the extent to which private property exists in society.

Industry is used here to mean the extent to which people are willing to work—to be industrious. It is not how hard you push it but how far you move it that counts. Nor is it the amount of time spent at the work site but how much is accomplished. Industry or work, then, is best thought of as effort applied to materials so as to produce what is wanted. Such industry is spiritual in that it is bent on accomplishment. It is that which leads to productivity.

Ingenuity is the applying of the mind to the task of production. It is the seeking of the most effective way to achieve results. The results of the free play of ingenuity is invention, the development of techniques, and the improvement of the devices of production.

The key to the American success story in productivity and material achievement lies in the discovery of those conditions that set the stage for and promote high incentives, industry, and ingenuity. This success is dependent upon the spirit of man being free that he may direct his energies toward constructive activity. The result is free enterprise.

The Constitution:
Limited Government and Free Men

The great breakthrough in America came with the adoption of the Constitution in 1787. During the Revolutionary War and the years immediately afterward, some state governments were especially irresponsible, if not oppressive. Thus, as many of those in the Constitutional Convention conceived the task, it was not only to provide for an effective general government but also to restrain the state goverments.

Their determination to limit and restrain those in government came out often in the debates during the Convention, as well as in letters and other papers of the period. In short, the new Constitution limited government and freed men. One of the best examples of this was in freeing commerce within the United States. For example, Congress is empowered "To regulate Commerce with foreign Nations, and among the several States, and with the Indian Tribes." To round this out, states are prohibited, "without the Consent of Congress, [to] lay any Imposts or Duties on Imports or Exports, except what may be absolutely necessary for executing its inspection laws...." The effect of these powers and restrictions was to make the United States a common market for trade within its bounds. This did much to free enterprise for Americans.

Two other provisions of the Constitution have been especially important for opening up the United States to trade throughout by all citizens. One is the provision for "uniform Laws on the subject of Bankruptcies throughout the United States." This meant inhabitants of a state could trade and make contracts in other states without fear that governments in those states could relieve their citizens of debts owed to outsiders. The other provision was the giving of power to Congress to issue patents and copyrights. This provided a common market throughout the United States in which inventors and authors could profit from their works.

Of more general importance was securing the country against the ravages of paper money. The Founders were quite familiar with the dangers of paper money. During the War for Independence, the Continental Congress issued increasingly large quantities of paper money (called "bills of credit" at that time) thus reducing or destroying the value of it as currency. States had not only issued such bills of credit during the war, but also some were flooding the market with it at the time of the Constitutional Convention.

71

So it was that the Founders placed in the Constitution a provision that "No State shall...coin Money; emit Bills of Credit; make any Thing but gold and silver Coin a Tender in Payment of Debts...."

Nor was any power granted to the United States government to issue paper money or bills of credit. The only provision regarding the currency in the Constitution is the one authorizing Congress "To coin Money, regulate the Value thereof, and of foreign Coin...." It was understood at the time that the United States government was one of delegated powers only, and that if a power were not granted to it by the Constitution it did not have any such power. We are not left in doubt in the case of a paper currency, however, for the matter was taken up during the Constitutional Convention, and resolved.

There was a move to carry over certain of the provisions of the Articles of Confederation in the Constitution, among them the one authorizing Congress to "emit bills of credit." It was moved and seconded that these words be deleted, and it was done by a vote of nine states to two. It was generally understood that the United States government would not have to issue paper money or make it legal tender. As James Madison wrote, he "became satisfied that striking out the words would...cut off the pretext for a paper currency, and particularly for making the bills a tender for public or private debts."

This elimination of unbacked (or unredeemable) paper currency was understood to be very important for long term contracts. If the government could issue paper money at will, those who had money owed to them would suffer as the value of the currency declined.

These various restrictions on governments highlight another aspect of the breakthrough with the United States government. The Americans may not have invented the idea of using a constitution as the law for governments, but they carried it through more thoroughly than any had done before. People generally are subject to ordinary laws in the course of their lives. Under our system, those who govern are placed under special laws. They are the restraints of constitutions. They limit government and free people generally.

One other protection from government needs to be especially emphasized. It is the protection of property, especially of private property. A number of the above-mentioned provisions are protections of property: for example, the protection of property in money by prohibiting bills of credit, or prohibiting the states to impair the obligation of contracts. But there are other more specific protections of property.

There are a number of protections of property in the Bill of Rights, or

First Ten Amendments. The most direct of these protections is in the Fifth Amendment, which provides that "No person shall be...deprived of life, liberty, or property, without due process of law; nor shall private property be taken for public use without just compensation." In brief, the police cannot simply seize property and keep it; only after full court procedures have been followed may property be taken. The Seventh Amendment protects property by requiring jury trial in all common lawsuits involving more than twenty dollars. The Fourth Amendment protects people's houses, papers, and effects from search and seizure, except for probable cause. The Fourteenth Amendment prohibits state governments to take life, liberty, or property without due process of law.

Most of the other restraints on government in the Constitution have at least a property dimension to them. For example, while we may not ordinarily think of the First Amendment restraints as property protection, they have that dimension as well. Even speech may be thought of as personal property, when a person delivers lectures, sermons, and other speeches, for which he may be paid (and if written down or otherwise recorded can be copyrighted). Freedom of the press is an empty right if one may not own a press as private property. In a similar fashion, without private property, the free exercise of religion might well be minus a place of assembly, Bible, hymnals, organs, and the various physical aids to worship.

The key to America's great productivity and material prosperity lies to a considerable extent in the political breakthrough which preceded it. The political breakthrough was a system of restraints upon government—laying down a law for governments, which is epitomized for us in the Constitution. The protection of private property provided maximum incentives, for it enabled people generally to keep most of what they produced or to dispose of it as they would. The restraints upon government freed men to direct their energy to production and make full and productive use of their ingenuity.

To see how all this worked, we must now look into some aspects of economics and economic development.

Employment

It is at the level of employment that we encounter the requirements of economics most directly and, sometimes, in the most pressing manner. Today, we hear much of unemployment. The Government attempts to count the employed and unemployed. Politicians of the party out of power belabor the extent of those unemployed, and we are taught to believe it is undesirable to be unemployed.

Basic to the consideration of employment is the understanding that everyone born on this planet has a ready-made job. This is not, perhaps, in the same sense that we usually refer to. Customarily we have in mind work associated with earning a living in a factory, office, store, mine, farm, or wherever. But if we look at the matter most basically we might see that what a man commonly refers to as his job is really the accidental work he happens to engage in, not his basic job. At least, it is not that job which all of us have to do to live on this planet. I am referring to the fact that each of us has to provide for his needs and wants. Indeed, our needs and wants appear as soon as we are born, long before we are able to supply them by our own labor. During the interval between maturity and infirmity, each of us has a job. Moreover, we may not only have the job of supplying our own needs and wants but also those of such others as become dependent upon us. This is our basic job.

It is the necessity of performing this job of supplying these needs and wants by work that makes employment desirable. Undoubtedly work may be good in many other ways; it is also a normal necessity.

It is easy enough to see, too, that to perform this job well we need the opportunity to keep a considerable portion of what we produce, i.e., have private property. Additionally, we need a great range of freedom to make the best and highest use of our time and energy.

Unemployment must be the result, then, either of obstacles being thrown in the way of our doing our job, the preference of leisure to work, or our needs and wants being supplied from other sources so that there is no necessity to work.

The Elements of Production

Production is the means by which our material wants and needs are satisfied. There are three basic elements of production of goods. They are: land, labor, and capital.

Land includes all the natural ingredients that may be used in material production. It includes the soil and all that may naturally grow out of it, the minerals on or within the earth, the water which lies beneath the soil or traverses it, and whatever else that we may think of as naturally being of the land. All those things that are commonly called natural resources are of the land. While natural resources do not account in themselves for the productive wealth of America, they are an essential ingredient in that production.

Labor includes all the human energy and ingenuity that go into the production of goods. Communists, and socialists more generally, often treat labor as if it involved only physical labor. Thus, they refer to industrial workers in factories as the "laboring class." Quite often farmers are excluded from "labor." In my opinion, treating "labor" this way is wrong. More properly, "labor" includes not only those who perform physical labor but also supervisors, managers, bookkeepers, salesmen, entrepreneurs (those who conceive and finance the whole enterprise), mechanics, and a great variety of others. In short, "labor" includes all those who use mind and body, skills and ingenuity, organizational and supervisory abilities, and in any way assist in the production of goods or the provision of services.

Capital is accumulated wealth which can be or is used in the production of more wealth. For example, a factory may be thought of as capital, and it will include buildings, machinery, equipment, all the devices used in production, and such raw materials as have been brought to the site for productive finishing. For example, lumber in stock at a woodworking plant would be capital. Operating capital may also include cash on hand or in reserve. Animals, such as horses and mules, were capital in times past, when they were used as beasts of burden. Today, they have been largely replaced in production by engines of one sort or another, and vehicles. Whether any particular good is capital, however, depends upon the use to which it is put rather than to what it is.

All the elements of production—land, labor, and capital—are scarce. This means that since they are capable of producing goods that are wanted, and since they are not available in unlimited quantities, they are scarce. They are not all scarce in the same degree, however; they are relatively scarce in relation to one another, and the degree of scarcity of one or the others will vary from time to time and place to place. In the early years of American development, land was relatively plentiful. Labor and capital were relatively scarcer. Thus, the mix of the elements of production will vary much from time to time. In an earlier America, for example, farmers used land much more freely—engaged in extensive rather than intensive cultivation—than labor or capital. In more recent times, capital has been much more extensively used in farming as well as for other undertakings.

The elements of production vary greatly in the extent to which they can be expanded. The supply of land on this planet is limited. New lands can be brought into cultivation, of course, and lands can be put to better or higher uses, but there is only so much land here. The supply of labor can be increased by increasing the birth rate and reducing the death rate. And the effectiveness of labor can be expanded by developing skills and habits of industriousness. Even so that which labor can produce is severely limited when machinery and other equipment is not used.

Potentially, the most expandable of the elements of production is technology—i.e., capital or the equipment and material used in production. We refer to these things as tools, the tools of production. By the use of tools, man can multiply the effect of his labor. Before expanding on the multiplier effect and describing ways in which Americans acting in freedom were able to expand their technology, we need to examine the role of the market in spurring production and distributing goods.

The Free Market

Earlier it was noted that every person has a job, that of supplying his needs and wants. In like manner, it can be said that every person has a market for what he might produce, that is, himself. Thus, in theory each person might have his own job of supplying his own goods for his own consumption. Then each of us would be a kind of Robinson Crusoe, an island to himself.

We would quickly discover, as Daniel Defoe's character, Robinson Crusoe, did that there are great difficulties in the way of being one's own supplier and market. There is nothing in the market except what one has produced. There are no tools except the crude ones we could contrive. We would always be limited to such skills as we could develop and to such things as we could produce from materials near at hand. Even one additional person, as Crusoe discovered, would greatly improve matters.

The market, or, since the word has been used in a strange sense thus far, the social market, is the great catalyst for production: that is, it provides the means for disposing of surplus produce, thus spurring production by offering a means of distribution. The market is the meeting place, any meeting place, for the exchange of goods, for the gathering of buyers and sellers. It makes possible specialization, by enabling a person to produce what he does best and exchanging it for goods that others have specialized in producing.

A free market is an even more wonderful contrivance. All peoples who have advanced beyond the most primitive or isolated stage will have some sort of market, but it may or may not be free. A free market is one in which buyers are free to offer their goods on whatever terms please them and trade only on terms that are mutually acceptable. To look at it more broadly, it is a market in which buyers can purchase the goods in whatever quality is acceptable on the best terms, because all buyers and sellers are in competition. If any authority intervenes to set prices or proclaim standards, it is not a free market. Choices are limited by such proclamations, and people are discouraged from operating in the market. Government is the great villain usually in hampering markets in this fashion. One of the great advantages of the restraints on government under the Constitution is the opportunity to have a free market.

The grease of the market is money, or medium of exchange. Markets exist without money, but trading by barter greatly hampers exchanges. Where barter is the mode, it is necessary to find someone who wants what you have to sell and who is offering what you would like to obtain. Even then, the exchange may not be made because of differences in value between the goods being offered, and the absence of any way to make change. A medium of exchange, a currency, or money, solves this problem. Indeed, money does more than provide a medium through which exchanges can be made; it provides a standard or measurement in which prices can be established. The market can only perform its full function by establishing the going prices for goods. Prices vary from time to time, depending upon the fluctuation of supply and demand, but at any time the going prices provide an invaluable standard for the making of exchanges.

Even so, the use of money in exchanges introduces a confusing element. A Frenchman, J. B. Say, pointed out early in the last century that, in effect, we always trade goods for goods. Money serves only as a medium through which to make exchanges, and it can be used to defer the completion of the transaction for other goods. But ultimately, he was saying, the transaction is completed with the purchase of goods or services. People often lose sight of this and suppose that wealth can be increased simply by increasing the supply of money. The result of acting on this belief, however, is only an increase of the medium—thus devaluing it—without increasing wealth in other goods. The Founders tried to guard against this by authorizing only the use of gold and silver as money.

The market (operating with sound money) offers a means for accumulating wealth. In economic terms, it provides an arena for the concentration of capital. Without markets, economic endeavor would be largely reduced to hand labor applied to land. The accumulation of wealth results from saving, and the market provides the arena within which surpluses can be disposed of and saving of money can occur. The market provides the means, then, for bringing the multiplier effect of technology into play.

Capital and Technology—The Multiplier Effect

The American success story could be told largely in terms of the increase, improvement, and use of evermore complex and effective tools. Tools are prime capital and the essence of technology. Thus, the American success story could be told in terms of technological development and capital expansion. But let us stick with tools for the moment.

Every instrument used in work from a pair of pliers to the most complex computer, can be thought of as a tool. Even the simplest of tools was once a marvelous invention. Most home garages have some basic tools: hammer, an axe, screwdrivers, a shovel, a wheelbarrow, a handsaw, and possibly a chain saw. While most of these tools are quite commonplace today, each in its own way illustrates the great advantage of tools. For example, try turning a screw without a screwdriver. It is not only rough going but very nearly impossible. Or, pick up dirt without a shovel. It can be done, but it is a slow go.

The usefulness of tools can be thought of, or described, in several ways. They are convenient. They are labor savers. They enable us to do things we would not otherwise find worthwhile or possible to do. They are man's helpers or assistants. Tools lengthen the arms of man, so to speak, increase his leverage, sharpen his teeth, give him more fingers, provide him with a cutting edge, etc. More importantly, tools enable man to multiply the effects of his efforts.

This multiplier effect can be illustrated by Eli Whitney's cotton gin, invented just a few years after the Constitution went into effect. Before Whitney's invention the only way to separate the cotton lint—the fibers—from the seed was by hand. One man manually turning Whitney's gin could do the work of 25 men who would otherwise separate the seeds from the lint by hand. This illustrates the multiplying effect of tools or machines.

It has often been charged, though, that there is an unpleasant side to the multiplying effect of machines, called technological unemployment. If one man with a cotton gin can do the work of 25 men, a logical conclusion is that 24 men would then be out of work. Literally, that might have been the result with the first few machines used, though it is unlikely that anyone wept over losing such tedious and laborious employment. Actually, very few people were employed full-time at separating lint from seeds by hand. Cotton was not used that much nor widely grown; it was too expensive. All that changed with the invention of the cotton gin. Many more people found employment as a result of the gin: growing cotton, ginning it, picking it, making it into yarn, weaving it into cloth, and so on. Cotton came into its own as a fiber, and many, even most, people could enjoy the soft cloth, and they did. Far from putting people out of work, cotton provided employment for millions of people by the middle of the 19th century.

So it is generally with the introduction of new technology. We all benefit through the variety and bounty of goods that result. Though some people may be displaced from a particular occupation, many others become employed in producing new and less costly products. The principle is that while human wants are insatiable, the means of satisfying them are limited. Technology not only provides many more choices in the market but also usually provides many more jobs than before. Technological unemployment is a misconception that human wants and the means of satisfying them are limited. In fact, the market can be greatly expanded with technology making more, better and less expensive products.

Inventions and the development of devices caused the great multiplication of production in the 19th and 20th centuries. Ingenuity provided the inventions; capital provided the means; and an expanding technology was the result. Limited government and free men provided the setting. The free market provided a way of accumulating savings and amassing wealth. Wealth provided the capital.

Much of the story of American progress in the 19th century can be told in terms of inventions and their development. Indeed, inventors came into their own for the first time in history, and some of them were as well or better known than politicians and generals. The name of Thomas A. Edison, for example, was better known than many of the nation's leaders in the latter part of the 19th century. The effects of the inventions of Eli Whitney, Robert Fulton, John Deere, Alexander Graham Bell, Henry Ford, Samuel F. B. Morse, and others are indelible.

Inventions in the 19th century included:

In the 1830s—the locomotive, reaper, electric motor, revolver, steel plow, and vulcanization of rubber.

In the 1840s—telegraph, turret lathe, sewing machine, rotary printing press, safety pin, and disc harrow.

In the 1850s—elevator, shoe sewing process, oil drilling process, Kelly process for converting iron to steel, and repeating rifle.

In the 1860s—Pullman sleeping car, ice making machine, revolving machine gun, and vacuum cleaner.

In the 1870s—streetcar, air brake, celluloid, calculators, motion pictures, dynamo, electric lights, and telephone.

In the 1880s—Phonograph, fountain pen, electric iron, roll film, and the safety bicycle.

Why was there such an outpouring of inventions during this relatively short period? There have been inventions from time to time over the thousands of years of recorded history, of course, but never, so far as we can judge, were so many of them made—and developed. Indeed, devices were invented in other periods of history, and many of them were never utilized or developed. For example, Leonardo da Vinci is believed to have made 21 inventions, which were soon forgotten.

The great differences lay in patent laws, capital, free enterprise, and energetic entrepreneurs. Patent laws protected inventors from imitators during the early years of development, thus making it profitable to introduce new inventions. The absence of government restraints on introducing new goods opened the way to their development. The security of property enabled people to accumulate funds for development.

The results, in large, were the multiplication of the energies of those who work with mind and body, a great increase in goods available to much larger populations, less expensive and often better goods, and the growing wealth of America.

Competition and Monopoly

The free market depends upon both monopoly and competition. Monopoly provides the goods for the market, and competition is the great regulator of the market.

Probably, no single term in economics has been more often misused or misunderstood than monopoly. In our era, monopoly has most often been pictured as an evil practice. It is true that general monopolies may be harmful, but private and limited monopolies such as those involved in private property and free labor are essential to both freedom and free enterprise.

Most basically, monopoly means an exclusive right of sale. It also means "the exclusive possession or control of something." Thus, all private property is a monopoly of its owner. It follows also that free labor involves an exclusive right to dispose of it. The free market depends upon the monoply of the owners of that which they sell or dispose in the market. Without such monopolies, there can be no real competition nor effective markets.

The dangers of monopoly arise when only one seller of a good or service is permitted to offer it in a particular market. Such monopolies usually arise when government gives special privileges to a particular seller, by way of franchises, licenses, or other grants of exclusive privileges. This removes all competition in that market for that particular good and places great power in the hands of the seller.

The ordinary corrective to private monopoly is competition. There is no danger in a free man having a monopoly of his own labor, so long as other men are free and may compete with him in the market. No one person can overcharge for his services for long in those circumstances, for others will enter the market to underbid him and keep the price at the market level. The same is true generally regarding the private ownership of goods. While private property does constitute a monopoly, so long as any producer can enter the market (and anyone is permitted to produce the goods), this monopoly provides little opportunity for price gouging or otherwise harming others.

Competition, then, is the great regulator in the market. Prices of goods are established in the market by competitive bidding. True, the ordinary sale of goods or services does not appear to be conducted as if it were an auction. Ordinarily, a person goes into a store and buys what he wants at the price marked on the items. In the case of high priced goods, such as an automobile, there may be some haggling over price, but for most consumer goods this does not occur directly. Even so, people do not always buy the goods, or unload the shelves of the grocery or department store at the marked prices. In these instances, the store operator may need to lower prices, hold a sale, or take what he can get for his goods. Also, people often go from store to store, comparing prices, and buying where they can get the best price for the quality they want or will accept. The merchant who sets his prices too high will have difficulty selling his goods. Other merchants will draw his customers. Thus, competition works to regulate the market for goods.

It is much the same with free labor in a free market. All workmen of similar skills and abilities are in competition with other workmen for jobs. In like manner, employers are in competition with one another for employees. In effect, labor (work) is sold in an auction. Again, that may not appear to be the case. Commonly, an employer announces the wage he will offer, and those who accept employment with him take the wage he has offered. In practice, however, workmen are often looking for better jobs and employers are looking for better workmen. Thus, workers take higher pay and better conditions generally when they are offered, and employers have to offer acceptable pay and other conditions to get or keep the number and quality of workers that he wants. Competition then regulates the conditions of labor in a free market.

Bountiful Consumer Goods

The ingredients discussed above—incentives, industry, and ingenuity, limited government and free men, free enterprise, savings, capital investment, the multiplier effect of technology, free markets, and competition—resulted in a bounty of goods from American productivity. Production does not exist for itself alone; the end of production is consumption. Prosperity is not measured simply by production but rather by better and less expensive goods in the hands of consumers. In large, that is the result in America.

By the last half of the 19th century, this result was almost everywhere in the country making itself felt. The figures for production of goods gives some indication of how many more goods were produced in the United States in 1900 than in 1850.

American farmers produced approximately 100,000,000 bushels of wheat in 1850; this had risen to 600 million by 1900. They produced 4,590,000 bales of cotton in 1850, and 10,226,000 in 1900. Corn production increased from 590 million bushels in 1850 to over 2.6 billion in 1900. The value of the annual product of manufacturing increased from approximately $2 billion in 1860 to $13 billion in 1900. This represented great increases in consumer goods. For example, in 1859, men's clothing manufacturers turned out a product worth over $73 million; in 1899, they made a product worth over $276 million. The worth of the factory produce for women's clothing was 20 times as great in 1899 as it was in 1859. Food manufacturers made similar increases. In 1849, flour and grist mill products were valued at approximately $136 million; in 1899, this had increased to about $560 million. Developments in transportation and communication were, if anything, more spectacular than those in manufacturing. The most remarkable of all was the development of rail transportation. In 1866, the rail mileage in the country was approximately 37,000 miles; by 1880, it had grown to 93,000 miles, and by 1890 to 163,000 miles. Even more remarkable perhaps were improvements made in trains to provide transportation for passengers and goods. No longer ago than 1840, say, there were those who feared that the human body could not withstand exposure to such speeds as 30 miles per hour. In 1893, a New York Central locomotive traveled at the speed of 120 miles per hour.

The important point of all this production of goods and provision of services, of course, is that these goods were going to more and more consumers. One indication of this is that production generally greatly outstripped the growth in population. The population of the United States slightly more than tripled during these years. It was 23,191,000 in 1850; by 1900 it was 75,994,000. Production of agricultural and manufacturing products was often five times or more in 1900 what it was in 1850. Moreoever, prices of goods generally declined over this period while per capita income increased. In terms of actual dollars, per capita income rose from $134 per year in 1859 to $185 in 1899. In terms of the goods the money would buy, the increase was from $285 to $488 between 1859 and 1914.

The miracle of production translated in prices was well described by Andrew Carnegie, the steelmaker, during the period:

> To make a ton of steel one and a half tons of iron stone has to be mined, transported by rail a hundred miles to the lakes, carried by boat hundreds of miles, transferred to cars, transported by rail one hundred and fifty miles to Pittsburg.... How then could steel be manufactured and sold without loss at three pounds for two cents? This, I confess, seemed to me incredible...but it was so.

This steel had hardly been available at all in 1850, and the price of what was, made such ordinary items as steel nails prohibitively expensive. By 1900, they were common building items for every man.

The Onslaught of Collectivism

Not everyone shared equally in the spreading prosperity that was the result of free enterprise. Some became quite wealthy; many prospered at more modest levels; others managed to get by generally, but were sometimes poor. These differences were hardly surprising in a society where each man's due was based on industry, ingenuity, and incentives. Men differ greatly in how hard and effectively they work, how well they manage their affairs, their willingness to save and invest, or their interests and aptitudes generally. Thus, it follows that if justice prevails, men will differ greatly in the rewards they receive. Even so conditions were improving generally. The United States was viewed as a land of opportunity, and immigrants from Europe poured into this country in increasing numbers in the latter part of the 19th century.

Yet the cry began to be heard from some that the system was wrong, that it must be either radically changed or modified. Ultimately, most of those who claimed this would favor the use of government to alter the system. There had never been a time when government had not intervened to some extent in the economy. But during the great era when the United States laid the foundation for prosperity, there was extensive free enterprise. As that system bore fruit, however, some began to clamor for government to play a much larger role in the economy. They were collectivists, as a rule, people who believed that productive enterprise should be publicly owned, managed, or controlled.

Although there was a considerable variety of collectivists in the last decades of the 19th century, they generally could be described as socialists. Socialists fell mostly into two categories eventually: revolutionary socialists and democratic socialists. The revolutionary socialists are best seen as Marxists—followers of Karl Marx. Marx was a German socialist (though he lived also in France and England), who wrote in the middle of the 19th century. He taught that socialism (or communism, as it came to be called) would come by way of revolution in all advanced countries. The rich would get rich and the poor poorer, he claimed, and eventually a great class struggle would bring revolution. The proletariat (working class) would rise up, seize the means of production, overturn the government, and issue in the classless society, where each would produce according to his ability and receive goods according to his needs. Government would wither away, and all men would be free.

Marx never lived to see any revolution which met his specifications. He did, however, attract some followers and left behind an assortment of writings which drew other disciples. Marxists and other socialist parties were formed, especially in Europe, and these worked to gain leverage, especially in labor unions. It was not in the advanced industrial countries of Europe or America that revolution took place, however. It was in more backward Russia in the early 20th century.

Democratic socialism has had a more checkered career. This variety of socialism is gradualist or evolutionary, does not propose to seize power all at once. Rather, such socialists proposed to move gradually toward their goal of government ownership or control over the economy. They are best exemplified by the Fabian Society in England. It was organized in 1884 and consisted mostly of writers and college people at first. They proposed to spread their ideas in existing organizations and move gradually toward political power. They made a large leap toward political power after World War I, by their influence in the newly organized Labor Party. The Labor Party was initially made up mostly of labor union people, but the Fabians succeeded in getting them to avow socialism as their goal.

The British Labour Party finally came to power near the end of World War II determined to carry through its socialist program. It did so with great vigor. Backbreaking taxes were levied on incomes; major industries were nationalized (taken over by the government); and a whole assortment of welfarist measures were passed, such as socialized medicine. The results were very nearly catastrophic. Britain's foreign trade was in deep trouble; the debt mounted; and even bread had to be rationed. Within a few years, the British were in retreat from such drastic policies, but it has been difficult to disentangle the economy from this huge assertion of government power.

Most of the countries of Europe, those not in the Soviet orbit, have made greater or lesser ventures into democratic socialism. However, there has been a definite aversion to government ownership of the means of production. Most democratic socialist countries have, instead, inclined more to favor government control over the economy to ownership and have involved themselves more or less heavily in welfarist measures. Sweden, which has experimented with democratic socialism even longer than Britain, definitely has favored government control and heavy taxation to taking over the industries. Such measures definitely hamper and distort economies, but they are neither so tyrannical nor harmful as government ownership.

Free Enterprise in America: Survival and Revival

American production has continued to grow in the 20th century. Indeed, after World War I, the United States emerged as the leading productive nation in the world. New inventions continued to come forth and be developed, quite often on a grand scale, such as the automobile, radio, refrigerator, movies, the airplane, television, and the great assortment of man-made wonders in this century.

Even so, the United States did not escape the surge of collectivism. By the late 19th century, there were outspoken socialists of a variety of flavors vying for American followers. Their views were cropping up in such political parties as the Populist and Socialist, and they were beginning to make inroads in the Democratic and Republican parties. Americans have always rejected socialism when it came under that label, and have given no significant vote to any such party since 1920. However, Americans have been drawn toward a variety of particular programs which are socialist in tendency or direction when they have been advocated by the leaders of the old parties.

The United States Constitution has been a major bulwark against collectivist practices. Granted, the Constitution can be amended, but mostly those bent on socializing America have not sought to reach their goal by constitutional amendments. The major exception to that was the adoption of the 16th Amendment in 1913. This allowed the government to impose an income tax, and before long the government began to impose a graduated tax. In general, though, American collectivists have gained such sway as they have by expanding the powers of the government through the interpreting of the Constitution and gradually extending its control over the economy.

The federal government began its thrust to control over the economy by the regulation of business. The regulation of banking began during the Civil War. The regulation of the railroads was begun by the Interstate Commerce Act in the 1880s, though much of the regulation now in effect came in the 20th century. The passage of the Federal Reserve Act in 1913, was a major move by the government toward the control over money. Business regulation was tightened by the anti-trust acts and by increasing the power and sway of the Interstate Commerce Commission. The Federal Trade Act extended government intervention in the economy.

In the 1930s the government moved headlong into efforts to plan the economy and redistribute the wealth. Government took over full control of the money and began the process of debasing the currency. Also, government became deeply involved in agriculture by crop controls, loans, and subsidies. High taxes tend to discourage, or make difficult, saving and investment. Incentives to production are reduced by progressive taxation: that is, when one earns more the government takes a larger percentage in taxes. Government increase of the money supply results in the decline of the value of money. When this happens, creditors are cheated by the declining value of the money they receive. Saving and investment are discouraged; spending is encouraged. Regulation of business makes it difficult for some to enter business and leads to rises in consumer prices. Then, instead of a free market, the result is a restricted and distorted market.

The United States has survived the onslaught of collectivism and remains as a land of opportunity and a haven from oppression. Most business in this country is still privately owned, though private property has suffered compromise as the result of extensive government controls. Through it all, a degree of freedom of enterprise has remained.

Socialism has been widely discredited. In general, its credit never was very high with Americans. The zeal has gone out of much of the push for government planning and ownership of the means of production in most of the advanced countries of the world. There remains, of course, in the United States and in other countries, a heavy crust of government programs, regulations, restrictions, and purported benefits of government spending. But the tide may be turning against collectivism and this trend will be fortified as today's Americans become more aware of the sources of the greatness of this nation.

SEPARATION OF CHURCH AND STATE

BY

ALBERT J. MENENDEZ

Edited by

WILLIAM G. SIZEMORE, 33°
(Rear Admiral, U.S.N., Ret.)

THE SUPREME COUNCIL, 33°
Ancient and Accepted Scottish Rite of Freemasonry
Mother Jurisdiction, U.S.A.
1733 16th Street, NW, Washington, DC 20009

W hat has been the most enduring achievement of the United States? The exploration of space? The assimilation of more than 50 million people from other lands and cultures? The development of a successful system of democratic government? A robust economy that has for most of its history assured the highest standard of living on earth to its citizens?

Or could it be something else? There are many who believe that the freedom to worship as one pleases—the right to believe, liberty of conscience—is the most significant contribution that this nation has made to the history and well-being of the world. "Religious freedom," wrote the late and beloved Senator Sam Ervin of North Carolina, "is America's most precious possession and must be preserved irrespective of its cost."

What does religious freedom mean? How did we achieve it? How should church and state relate in a nation which constitutionally separates them for the good of both and for the preservation of the common good? Why are the courts called upon to resolve church-state disputes so frequently in recent years? These are some of the questions this article will try to answer.

Religous liberty means more, much more, than just the right to worship at the religious edifice of one's choice. A group of religious leaders working to make the American ideal a universal one arrived at a definition that seems to be comprehensive. In 1978 the group called Freedom of Faith issued this statement of principles. To be complete, religious liberty had to include the following religious rights:

1. Every person has the right to determine his or her own faith and creed according to conscience.
2. Every person has the right to the privacy of his belief, to express his religious beliefs in worship, teaching, and practice, and to proclaim the implications of his beliefs for relationships in a social or political community.
3. Every person has the right to associate with others and to organize with them for religious purposes.
4. Every religious organization, formed or maintained by action in accordance with the rights of individual persons, has the right to determine its policies and practices for the accomplishment of its chosen purposes, which implies the right:
   a. to assemble for unhindered private or public worship.
   b. to formulate its own creed.
   c. to have an adequate ministry.

d. to determine its conditions of membership.
e. to give religious instruction to its youth, including preparation for ministry.
f. to preach its message publicly.
g. to receive into its membership those who desire to join it.
h. to carry on social services and to engage in missionary activity both at home and abroad.
i. to organize local congregations.
j. to publish and circulate religious literature.
k. to control the means necessary to its mission and to secure support for its work at home and abroad.
l. to cooperate and to unite with other believers at home and abroad.
m. to use the language of the people in worship and in religious instruction.
n. to determine freely the qualifications for professional leadership of religious communities, freely naming their religious leaders at all levels and designating their work assignments.

These many components of religious freedom have taken decades, even centuries, to refine because those who initially settled this country did not often wish to accord full religious rights to opposing or minority religions.

The early English, Scottish, German, French and Spanish colonists who settled and explored what is now the USA had a very limited understanding of religious freedom or religious tolerance. They came from societies dominated by a single religious tradition, and they found it difficult to extend the full protection of the law to dissenters. Even those dissenters who fled their European homelands to seek a place to worship freely did not generally extend the same freedom to others. Thus, nine of the thirteen British colonies had established churches on the eve of the American Revolution.

Before the Constitution granted an unprecedented measure of religious freedom to United States citizens, there were many individuals who paved the way.

Two of the earliest declarations of support for freedom of conscience were Maryland's 1649 Act of Toleration and the 1657 Flushing Remonstrance.

On April 21, 1649, the legislators of the Maryland colony, meeting in St. Mary's City, approved an Act Concerning Religion. This little noticed piece of legislation was quite advanced for its time, because it committed the civil authorities to a position of neutrality with regard to the various

Christian denominations and used the term "free exercise" of religion, possibly for the first time in our country. One provision stipulated that "Nor shall any be compelled to the belief or exercise of any other religion against his or her consent." The Act was not perfect, as it excluded Jews and other non-Christians from its protection. Yet, in an age when the vast majority of the people were either Protestant or Catholic, it provided for religious tolerance for the vast majority of Christian believers.

A unique aspect of the Maryland Act was that a considerable portion of the Maryland colony, including its proprietors, were members of the Roman Catholic Church. No reliable data is available on the members of the General Assembly, but at least a third, if not half, of the courageous legislators who voted for the Act were Catholics.

Dutch colonists settled in what is now New York State in 1624. The merchant class, which predominated in the new colony, was more concerned with economic progress than religious polemic, so for most of the next 40 years there was a great degree of religious tolerance in the New Netherland colony, though the Reformed Church was theoretically the established church. Some authorities have claimed there was more freedom in the colony than in the mother country. However, an inevitable conflict occurred between the clergy, who wanted to crush dissent, and the merchants. In 1650 the Charter of Freedoms and Exemptions stated that "No other religion shall be publicly admitted in New Netherland except the Reformed." It appears that this attempt at repression was not widely enforced until the legendary Peter Stuyvesant became governor in the 1650s.

Stuyvesant's religious ire was vented at an obscure little group of tolerant, peaceful dissenters, the Society of Friends, or Quakers. Anson Phelps Stokes claimed that Stuyvesant disliked Quakers because "Their street meetings and disregard of authority offended him." In August 1657 a Quaker preacher, Robert Hodgson, held a number of successful meetings in English communities under Dutch jurisdiction on Long Island. At the order of the governor he was arrested and subjected to great cruelty, almost dying from prolonged whippings. Stuyvesant's sister, Emma, pleaded with the governor so fervently that he released Hodgson from a death sentence on condition that he leave New Netherland forever.

In the fall of 1657 Stuyvesant issued a proclamation whereby any ship bringing a Quaker into the province of New Netherland would be liable to confiscation. Any citizen harboring a known Quaker overnight would be subject to a fine of L50, half of which was to go to the informer. This decree was received obediently in most parts of the province, except for one area, the town of Flushing on Long Island. The inhabitants of Flushing, mostly English settlers who had fled religious persecution in New England, founded the town in 1645 and explicitly included "liberty of conscience" in the town charter of 1645. The inhabitants had been involved in a running battle with Stuyvesant for over a decade about the tolerance of the town for all religious opinions.

Citing the "Freedom from Molestation" clause of the 1645 charter, the inhabitants of Flushing rose up in indignation against Stuyvesant's ordinance against Quakers. Under the aegis of the sheriff, Tobias Feake, a "remonstrance" was drawn up, signed by 31 townsmen and presented to the governor. This document, known now as the "Flushing Remonstrance," is a remarkable and eloquent defense of liberty of conscience. The free men proclaimed that they would welcome "any sons of Adam who came in love among us," and would not "condemn, punish, banish, prosecute or lay violent hands upon anyone, in whatever name, form or title he might appear." The Remonstrance claimed that "We are true subjects both of the church and the state," but "we are bound by the law of God and man to do good unto all men, and evil to no man...."

Roger Williams

Though neither of the above acts created permanent religious freedom in Maryland or New York, they were milestones on the road to liberty. A contemporary event was the founding of Rhode Island by religious reformer Roger Williams. Though born in England, Williams sought greater personal freedom and migrated to Boston in 1631. He opposed the religious establishment there and sought to establish an enclave of freedom in Rhode Island. In his 1640 classic *The Bloody Tenet of Persecution,* he maintained that "civil weapons are most improper and unfitting in the matters of the spiritual state," and that constraint engendered hypocrisy. If a state were to force people to be good Christians, this would remove the voluntary commitment element essential for Christianity. Also, persecution in the name of religion would destroy the integrity of the church.

Williams placed his revolutionary concept of freedom into the civil code of his colony in 1647, and complete liberty of conscience was granted here for the first time in western civilization.

He further developed a concept of church-state relations which would ultimately lead to the separation which we in America now enjoy. He espoused the "remnant" theory of ecclesiology. He believed that true Christians would always be a minority in any society. He wrote: "The state includes everybody in a given area. The church comprises only the regenerate and they are bound to be few and incompatible with the world which will certainly subject them to persecution."

In 1654 Williams wrote the famous letter on religious freedom in which he compared the world to a ship in which people of many faiths and traditions must, for a time, live in harmony.

Roger Williams may not have realized it at the time, but he was a trailblazer in man's long and difficult struggle for religious freedom. His little colony in the wilderness of a new land in the 17th century proved to be a tremendous and far-reaching experiment. Williams' monumental contribution to religious liberty was hailed by professor Georg Jellinek of the University of Heidelberg, Germany, in 1901:

"The idea of legally establishing inalienable, inherent and sacred rights of the individual is not of political but of religious origin. What has been held to be a work of the Revolution was in reality a fruit of the Reformation and its struggles. Its first apostle was not Lafayette but Roger Williams, who, driven by power and deep religious enthusiasm, went into the wilderness in order to found a government of religious liberty, and his name is uttered by Americans even today with the deepest respect."

Other important figures in the freedom struggle include the dissenter Anne Hutchinson, the magistrate Thomas Hooker, and an ordained Presbyterian minister, Samuel Davies, who spoke out on behalf of religious minorities in Virginia.

William Penn

Another trailblazer in the struggle for religious freedom was William Penn. Penn, born in 1644 of a prominent family, was an independent thinker and, while a student at Oxford, embraced the recently founded group known as the Society of Friends (derisively called "Quakers" by the establishment). Young William found himself in jail for his unorthodox religious views and in this crucible was formed his deep conviction that the state must not defend or repress any religious sentiment. He was a prolific writer, and published the *Great Case of Liberty of Conscience* in 1670. Like Roger Williams before him, Penn proposed that government maintain a hands-off policy towards religion.

Penn sought religious freedom for his co-religionists and hoped to obtain a grant from the king for a colony in the New World. In 1676 he drew up his *Concessions,* a proposed constitution for his colony. He provided for absolute religious freedom and hoped to establish "a free colony for all mankind." Penn was a co-proprietor of the tiny colony of West Jersey, but it attracted only a handful of settlers. The charter for West Jersey, however, was, in Leo Pfeffer's words, "a great forward step in the history of civil liberty, providing as it did not only for liberty of conscience, but also for security from illegal arrests, trial by jury, and control of taxation by representatives elected by secret ballot of the entire body of the proprietors, freeholders, and inhabitants of the colony."

Penn finally received his charter from King Charles II in 1681 and established for the new colony of Pennsylvania a provision for religious freedom. This constitution, called the Great Law of 1682, provided that no person "shall in any case be molested or prejudiced for his or her conscience, persuasion or practice. Nor shall he or she at any time be compelled to frequent or maintain any religious worship, place or ministry whatever...." Interestingly, the law provided penalties for any individual who "abuse or deride" other individuals for religious reasons. The law provided that "such a person should be looked upon as a disturber of the peace and punished accordingly." For the late 17th century this was a remarkable document, especially since the Edict of Nantes had recently been revoked by France and thousands of protestants were either imprisoned or had to flee from their country once again. By today's standards Penn's constitution was not perfect, as it provided that only Christians could hold public office. In addition, blasphemy was a civil crime and Sunday observance was rigidly enforced.

William Penn's contribution to the development of religious freedom cannot be underestimated. As Anson Phelps Stokes wrote in *Church and State in the United States,* "He took the ground that church government was no part of political government; that persecutors were never in the right; that a clear distinction must be made between the things that belong to Caesar and those that belong to God, and that the spirit of tolerance was a form of respect for the individual which was of the very essence of the Christian message."

At the time of American independence, a remarkable group of statesmen interested themselves in the cause of religious freedom. Their influence significantly affected the victorious outcome of the struggle.

James Madison

James Madison, "the father of the constitution," was a Virginian Episcopalian who early saw the evils of religious establishments, even when the established church was his own. "Ecclesiastical establishments tend to great ignorance and corruption," he wrote.

Believing that "the right of every man is to liberty" and not merely to toleration, Madison was successful in getting the word "toleration" in the 1776 Virginia Bill of Rights modified to read "all men are equally entitled to the free exercise of religion, according to the dictates of conscience." One scholar has stated that this clause of Madison's asserted "for the first time in any body of fundamental law, a natural right which had not previously been recognized as such by political bodies in the Christian world."

After the American Revolution, Patrick Henry and other legislators proposed a bill to require all Virginia taxpayers to support "teachers of the Christian religion."

Madison saw the dangers in this proposal when he wrote, "It is proper to take alarm at the first experiment on our liberties." Madison, as a member of the House of Delegates of Virginia, drew up a "Memorial and Remonstrance Against Religious Assessments" which has remained for two centuries one of the most explicit and eloquent warnings against church-state entanglement.

Madison wrote, "We hold it for fundamental and undeniable truth that religion, or the duty which we owe our Creator, and the manner of discharging it, can be directed only by reason and conviction, not by force or violence. The religion, then, of every man must be left to the conviction and conscience of every man; and it is the right of every man to exercise it as these may dictate."

Madison warned that "The same authority which can establish Christianity, in exclusion of all other religions, may establish with the same ease any particular sect of Christians in exclusion of all other sects." He used history to strengthen his argument. "Torrents of blood have been spilled in the old world in consequence of vain attempts of the secular arm to extinguish religious discord by proscribing all differences in religious opinion." Ecclesiastical establishments, "instead of maintaining the purity and the efficacy of religion," actually led to "ignorance, servility, superstition, bigotry and persecution."

One of Madison's biographers expressed the significance of this event when he wrote that "this was indeed his great contribution to the cause of religious liberty—that he looked beyond the seemingly trivial levy in the aid of religious teachers, and saw its ultimate consequence in the denial of liberty and imposition of clerical control upon the state."

As a sidelight to history, it is instructive to consider the influence of two ministers on the philosophical development and public career of James Madison. John Witherspoon, a Scottish Presbyterian clergyman and educator was president of the College of New Jersey (now Princeton) when young James Madison came to study. Witherspoon, who taught that "the only proper principle for a republic" is "complete liberty of worship," is credited with helping to shape Madison's views on the proper relationship between church and state.

Witherspoon's influence was paramount in New Jersey's rejection of religious assessments and establishments. The great historians Samuel Eliot Morison and Henry Steele Commager in *The Growth of the American Republic* memorialized the great Presbyterian divine's achievements: "He was forever preaching that mere toleration was not enough, for that implied superiority and condescension; the only proper principle for a republic was complete liberty to worship how one chose or not at all, and every church should be supported by its own members or funds without help from the taxing power of the state. Witherspoon's pupils, among whom James Madison was conspicuous, were always to be found on the side of religious liberty."

John Leland, an influential Baptist preacher in Orange County, Virginia, besieged the Virginia Establishment with pleas for religious freedom. Leland, though he appreciated James Madison's efforts to secure passage to Thomas Jefferson's "Bill for Establishing Religious Freedom," announced his candidacy for the convention which would decide whether Virginia would ratify the proposed Federal Constitution. Leland feared that a Bill of Rights, guaranteeing religious and civil liberty would not be included in the Constitution. Madison was vigorously campaigning for ratification, and Virginia was the key state. Leland's popularity was considerable and Madison's election was not certain. Leland met Madison and, though no records exist, an agreement must have resulted. Leland withdrew, insuring Madison's election. Madison led the ratification forces to a slim victory and soon after won a seat in the new congress, where he proposed the adoption of a Bill of Rights.

Three other statesmen, whose contributions to American political history are almost inestimable also lent their voices to the religious liberty movement. President George Washington believed that all people, regardless of belief, should be treated equally before the law and that "bigotry" should be given "no sanction" by government. Benjamin Franklin recognized the importance of the voluntary principle in religion. George Mason, an Episcopal vestryman, was primary author of the Virginia Declaration of Rights and an advocate of "the fullest toleration in the exercise of religion."

Before we discuss the profound importance of the First Amendment, tribute should be paid to four less well-known figures. Isaac Backus was a Baptist theoretician whose lucid and articulate writings helped to shape the intellectual arsenal of religious libertarians. Two Episcopalian public servants led the fight against the imposition of any religious test for public office: Charles Pinckney of South Carolina proposed that "no religious test shall ever be required as a qualification to any office or public trust under the United States" (which became Article VI of the U.S. Constitution); Samuel Livermore, a New Hampshire congressman, made the original "motion" which embodied the proposal debated by Congress in drafting the First Amendment. Thomas Kennedy, a Presbyterian, led a long fight in the Maryland legislature on behalf of Jewish civil rights, which finally resulted in the passage of an 1825 bill granting equal rights under the law to Jewish citizens of the "Free State."

The most important landmark in the ceaseless struggle for religious freedom has surely been Article I of the Bill of Rights of the United States Constitution. Sixteen succinct words, "Congress shall make no law respecting an establishment of religion, or prohibiting the free exercise thereof" represent the concrete realization of centuries of unfulfilled dreams. A bulwark of liberty and a protection against governmental repression, the First Amendment was clearly intended to erect, as Jefferson said, "a wall of separation between church and state."

As we face the future as a nation, we must rebuild the spirit of liberty. We cannot expect the Supreme Court or Congress to solve all church-state disputes. Nor can we expect impersonal institutions to preserve religious freedom in times which are rapidly changing.

Historian Glenn T. Miller in *Religious Liberty in America,* summed up our challenge: "The definition of religious freedom is in a continual process of flux. What we make of that freedom and the traditions which sustain it is our own choice. Ultimately, after the arguments of political scientists and constitutional experts are in, it is the living experience of Americans that determines what freedom means. All the formal protections of liberty are meaningless statements of principles unless we create a society that nourishes freedom and guarantees its expression. The Supreme Court may be as strict as it pleases, but if the American people themselves do not eradicate the often hidden social forces that make freedom meaningless, then we will have tyranny. The only revolution that lasts is not the one on the battlefield, but the one in the hearts and the minds of the people."

THE THREAT OF
COMMUNIST EXPANSIONISM

BY

BENJAMIN WYLIE TARWATER, 33°
(Colonel, USAF, Ret.)

THE SUPREME COUNCIL, 33°
Ancient and Accepted Scottish Rite of Freemasonry
Mother Jurisdiction, U.S.A.
1733 16th Street, NW, Washington, DC 20009

World War II could have been prevented if the "Allied" countries had understood the objectives, ethics and morals, and strategy and tactics of the "Axis" countries—and had taken appropriate preventative action. We, and the other non-communist nations of the world can continue our ways of life, prevent a Communist-initiated World War III, and prevent the success of Communist led revolutions throughout the world, if we understand Communist objectives, ethics, morals, strategy and tactics—and if we take appropriate preventative action.

Unfortunately, as of this writing, many patriotic Americans in government, the media, and elsewhere, seriously disagree as to the nature of the Communist threat. Some believe the problem is global, involving the Marxist-Leninists in most of the countries of the world. They hold that the Communists have never stopped waging the cold war and that Communism is a mortal threat to our way of life. Others believe that those holding these views have an inordinate fear of Communism, that the Communists truly believe in "peaceful coexistence," as we understand the meaning of these words, and that the actions of the leading and most powerful Communist nation, the Soviet Union, are essentially motivated by understandable national interests and superpower competition with the United States.

This disagreement prevents us from having bipartisan foreign and military policies not only in Central America but throughout the world. So, our problem is to determine what the problem is—for as a wise person has said: "If we could agree on where we want to go, we would have a better chance of getting there."

In an effort to help provide the needed understanding of the problem, this paper focuses on Communist expansionism. It describes Marxist-Leninist beliefs and how they impact on Communist objectives, ethics and morals, and strategy and tactics. It answers specific questions on the nature of the Communist threat and provides conclusions along with recommended actions.

Key Communist Beliefs

Extensive research, and many years of observing Communist strategy and tactics, reveals that the key to understanding and believing the true nature of the Communist problem, is to understand Marxism-Leninism. In fact, all Marxist-Leninists throughout the world will agree with Leonid Brezhnev's statement that "Marxism-Leninism is a coherent international teaching, it is a theory which belongs to all Communists and all revolutionaries and serves them as a guide to action."[1] All Marxist-Leninists will also agree with the statement that "the indestructible foundation of the whole edifice of Marxism-Leninism is its philosophy—dialectical and historical materialism."[2] As a result a review of the Communists' philosophy and how it impacts on their objectives, ethics, morals, strategy and tactics is a logical and necessary beginning.

As materialists, the Communists believe there is no God, no eternal moral principles; only matter is real. They believe that movement is an inherent part of all matter, and that matter moves in accordance with the laws of dialectics.

Some of the important concepts of the laws of dialectics include: (1) every phenomenon is in a constant state of change due to inherent internal contradictions, and the effect of all surrounding phenomena acting upon it, for everything is interconnected and interrelated, (2) all phenomena are a temporary unity of opposites, thesis and antithesis, changing from the old disintegrating and dying thesis, to the new arising and developing synthesis, (3) the unity of all phenomena is temporary, whereas their change is constant, with gradual quantitative changes building to a point of revolutionary intensity, and then (differing from evolution) there is a revolutionary "leap" from the old phenomenon to a qualitatively new phenomenon, and (4) each qualitatively new phenomenon arising in its turn goes through the same process of quantitative to qualitative change. Consequently, the universe consists of an endless progression of matter in motion, ever changing from one qualitative form to another.

Applying this concept to history the Marxist-Leninists believe the Earth started as a molten mass and that matter then moved dialectically, progressing from the inanimate to the animate—to the highest form of matter, matter which thinks—the brain. And they believe that since people are simply matter, people and civilizations also move in accordance with the laws of dialectics.

Marxist-Leninists believe that during the course of history civilization has passed through four major stages or eras. They believe the most significant feature of each of these stages has been the conflict between the two major economic classes, which are the primary "thesis" and "antithesis" of each major historical era. There are other less important "thesis-antithesis" cycles going on at the same time. But the major contradiction during each historical era is the conflict between those that own the means of production, the exploiters, and those that do not, the exploited.

The Communists believe that the first historical period was a "classless-communal" era; that this was followed by the master-slave era, with the masters being the "thesis" and the slaves the "antithesis." Then, as the means of production changed, contradictions and antagonisms between the masters and the slaves (and in the whole superstructure of society) developed to a point of revolutionary intensity. There was an upheaval resulting in a synthesis, and a new era of civilization resulted—the lord-serf relationship, with the lords and serfs becoming the new "thesis" and "antithesis." Then, as the means of production again changed and the antagonisms and contradictions between these economic classes (and in the whole superstructure of society) grew to revolutionary intensity, there was another upheaval, resulting in the worker-capitalist era.

In accordance with Lenin's teachings the Marxist-Leninists believe that the worker-capitalist era has reached its final stage, Imperialism. "Imperialism is decaying and moribund capitalism; it is the eve of the socialist revolution. The world capitalist system as a whole is ripe for the social revolution of the proletariat."[3]

On the basis of their dialectical materialist interpretation of history they predict and believe that Communist "revolutions" or "just wars" will end the worker-capitalist era. This will be followed by a transition period during which, the "vanguard of the proletariat," the Communist party members, will impose a Communist party dictatorship that will "smash" the non-Marxist-Leninist "socio-economic formations," eliminate the remnants of capitalist and individualist thinking, build socialism, and eventually a developed Communist society will emerge.

Then "on condition that (Marxist-Leninist) socialism triumphs and is consolidated in the international arena,"[4] after our way of life and other non-Communist ways of life have been destroyed, there will no longer be "exploitation of man by man," human nature will change, and each person "prompted by only moral stimuli" will contribute "in accordance with his ability and receive in accordance with his needs," and "the state will wither away."

Additionally, the Marxist-Leninists believe that some people's brains have developed dialectically more than others. These people have "advanced consciousness" which enables them to understand and act in accordance with Marxist-Leninist theory. Consequently, these people in the various countries of the world, are supposed to be identified, educated and trained in Marxism-Leninism and organized into "iron disciplined" Communist parties. These parties are "the vanguard of the world revolutionary movement." They provide the leadership in the Marxist-Leninist efforts to destroy all non-Communist ways of life and to build Communism.

"The principle task of the Communist parties...is to unite the scattered Communist forces, to form in every country a united Communist party...in order to increase tenfold the work of preparing the proletariat for the conquest of political power...."[5]

Under the conditions of Imperialism, the Communist parties are free to seize power anytime the correlation of forces enables them to gain power and to retain it. They do not have to wait for a country or the world to pass through all the historical eras set forth by Marx and Engels. "The task and art of Communist leaders lies in correctly gauging the conditions and the moment when the vanguard of the proletariat can successfully seize power, when it will be able, during and after this seizure of power, to obtain adequate support from a sufficiently broad strata of the working class and of the non-proletarian toiling masses, and when thereafter, it will be able to maintain, consolidate and extend its rule...."[6]

We should also be aware that even though the correlation of forces in some countries is such that the Communist party members cannot immediately seize power, they believe they should support revolutions "against the social and political order of things" (as in Iran), including wars of "National Liberation" in Asia, Africa and Latin America, because they weaken and undermine global Imperialism "facilitating its overthrow."

The Marxist-Leninist beliefs that have been described are the foundation of the Communists: (1) Objectives—destruction of all non-Communist ways of life and the establishment of world Communism, (2) Ethics and Morals—anything that speeds the destruction of non-Communist ways of life and the establishment of world Communism is ethical and moral, and (3) Strategy and Tactics—which start with a total dialectical analysis of the changing historical context, then they determine the correlation of forces (comparative weaknesses and strengths) and all the forces at work within the objective and acting upon it from the outside. Then on the basis of the insights provided by the dialectical analysis they determine their specific strategy and tactics.

Strategy and Tactics

Communist strategy and tactics benefit from the fact that, consistent with their fundamental Marxist-Leninist beliefs, they have constant, unchanging, dynamic objectives; destruction of all non-Communist Governments, and the imposition of Communist party dictatorships throughout the world.

The Marxist-Leninist strategy and tactics also benefit from the fact that, consistent with their beliefs, they can take any action without being inhibited by moral constraints as we know them. They believe that anything, repeat, anything that speeds the destruction of non-Communist Governments and the establishment of world Communism is ethical and moral. Failure to take advantage of any opportunity to speed the destruction of non-Communist ways of life and to speed the establishment of world communism, is unethical and immoral. In other words, friendly "bear hugs" or verbal venom and promises to "bury us," lies or truth, legal or illegal actions, cold war or detente, war or peace, any of these actions is ethical and moral if the total gains for establishing Communism outweigh the total costs.

Consistent with their theory, the Marxist-Leninists use a four-step method of analysis and planning to determine their strategy and tactics for different forms of direct military aggression, as well as for psychological, economic, political, diplomatic and other forms of indirect aggression:

First, they make a total dialectical analysis of their objective in light of their interpretations of changing historical contexts. They consider all the forces at work within their objective and the forces acting upon it from the outside—whether their immediate objective is a country, a group of countries, an institution, a group, or an individual. They identify weaknesses or potential weaknesses which can be exploited to serve their purpose.

"The demand for 'all-sided study' evolves from the fundamental principle of Marxist-Leninist philosophy about the unity of the world and universal interrelations, the mutual dependence of objects and phenomena of nature and society. It consists in the analysis of the entire aggregate of the links and relations of every object, every phenomenon and process with other objects, phenomena and processes. In order really to know an object it is necessary to embrace, to study all its aspects, all its links and 'mediacies.' Although this can never be achieved in full measure, the emphasis on all-sided study helps to avoid errors and rigid attitudes. This demand finds its concrete expression in the Marxist-Leninist approach to war, which is regarded in all its aspects, in connection with its socioeconomic and political sources and causes, in the unity of the armed struggle and the economic, ideological and diplomatic forms of warfare."[7]

Second, depending upon the results of the dialectical analysis of the "correlation of forces" (the comparative weaknesses and strengths of their adversaries), they determine the "form(s) of struggle." These can be ideological, psychological, political, economic, diplomatic, military, legal or illegal, peaceful or non-peaceful or any other form(s) which they believe will be most effective in exploiting their objective at that particular time.

"Marxism unconditionally demands that the question of the forms of struggle should be examined historically. He who considers this question without relation to the concrete historical situation, does not understand the A-B-C of dialectical materialism. At different moments of economic evolution, and depending on varying political, national, cultural, and other social conditions, different forms of struggle assume prominence, become the chief forms of struggle, whereupon, in their turn, the secondary and supplementary forms of struggle also change their aspect. He who endeavors to accept or reject a definite means of struggle without a detailed examination of the concrete conditions of the given moment at the given stage of its development, has entirely abandoned Marxist ground."[8]

"The Communist and workers' parties are conducting their activity in diverse specific conditions, requiring an appropriate approach to the solution of concrete problems. Each party, guided by the principles of Marxism-Leninism and in keeping with concrete national conditions, fully independent, elaborates its own policy, determines the directions, forms and methods of struggle and, depending on the circumstance, chooses the peaceful or non-peaceful way of transition to socialism...."[9] *(The Marxist-Leninist Form* of socialism is considered to be the first phase of communism.)

Concerning choosing direct military aggression, or war, as the form of struggle, Lenin said: "If war is waged by the Proletariat after it has conquered the bourgeoisie in its own country, and is waged with the object of strengthening and extending socialism, such a war is legitimate and holy."[10] "...as soon as we are strong enough to defeat Capitalism as a whole, we shall immediately take it by the scruff of the neck."[11] "When one enjoys an overwhelming superiority of forces one can succeed by a direct frontal attack. When forces are inadequate, detours, waiting periods, zigzags, retreats, and so on and so forth, may be necessary."[12]

(Comment: Since, up to this time, the Communists have not attempted to "take us by the scruff of the neck," it is obvious that they have concluded from their analysis that the total gains of a direct frontal attack would not be worth the total costs. It is apparent, however, that they are trying to develop a comparative military superiority which would enable them to intimidate, coerce and possibly get non-Communists to give up or surrender without a fight—"...realizing the hopelessness of resistance...,"[13] or failing this, military superiority would enable them to prevail in a military conflict.

At the same time that they are building their strength, they are using various forms of struggle to weaken the will and capability of the non-

Communists to resist. This includes such things as: Supporting any revolutionary activity that may result in our being denied essential raw materials or strategic position; trying to break up or weaken remaining non-Communist collective defense arrangements like NATO and ANZUS; trying to get us to agree to nuclear free zones, or a nuclear freeze or a disarmament agreement that will lessen our capability to deter them from attempting coercion or from trying to take us "by the scruff of the neck.")

Concerning spreading revolution, Lenin said that after seizing power in a country, the Communists in that country should do "a maximum of what is feasible in one country in order to develop, to support, to arouse the revolution in all countries."[14] "As long as we have not conquered the whole world, as long as, from the economic and military standpoint, we are weaker than the capitalist world, we must adhere to the rule that we must know how to take advantage of the antagonisms and contradictions existing among the Imperialists."[15] "It is possible to conquer the more powerful enemy only by exerting the utmost effort, and by necessarily, thoroughly, carefully, attentively and skillfully taking advantage of every, even the smallest fissure among the enemies, antagonism of interest among the bourgeoisie in the various countries, among the various groups or types of bourgeoisie in the various countries; by taking advantage of every, even the smallest opportunity of gaining a mass ally, even though this ally be temporary, vacillating, unstable, unreliable and conditional."[16] "In all organizations without exception—unions and associations, primarily proletarian, and also organizations of the non-proletarian, toiling and exploited masses (political, industrial, military, cooperative, educational, sports, etc.), groups or nuclei of Communists should be formed—mainly open groups, but also secret groups, ...carrying on work of agitation propaganda and organization...."[17]

In considering indirect aggression forms of struggle, it is important to understand that while the Communists have declared their intention to seize power and impose Marxist-Leninist rule on every country in the world, they do not openly "declare war" against specific countries. They just start what can be described as termite operations. Like termites they gnaw away at the strength of non-Communist structures. In individual nations these termite operations are a form of conspiratorial internal aggression, spearheaded by native Marxist-Leninist "termites" who are nurtured from the main "nests," the countries already under Marxist-Leninist control. In these termite operations the native Marxist-Leninists use ideological, psychological and political forms of struggle in efforts to confuse and divide the non-Communists and cause them to lose confidence in their non-

Communist institutions, policies and leaders. Economically and militarily they work to weaken the non-Communists' capability and will to resist the Communists. When the Communists use force, beyond terrorism, such as guerilla warfare, the termite operations continue. At this point the education, training, and material support provided by the "nurturing nests," such as the Soviet Union and Cuba, is greatly increased. In addition, these Communist nations take psychological and diplomatic actions in the international arena generally designed to convince the world that the Communist guerillas, or whatever, are waging a just conflict against an unjust, corrupt and cruel regime.

In conducting their strategy and tactics the Communists cleverly exploit the non-Communists' desire for international morality and law and order in ways designed to prevent, or hobble, opposition from the non-Communist world. For example, in their attempts to seize power in individual countries they wrap their internal aggression in the cloak of native "reform" movements until they are firmly in power. Then the cloak gradually slips away and reveals that the dominant members of the "reform" movement are in fact Marxist-Leninists, sharing the same philosophy, the same objectives, the same ethics and morals and the same method of planning as their allies and coconspirators in the Soviet Union and the other Communist countries.

Third, after determining the form of struggle they decide on the things they will have to accomplish, and the necessary sequence for accomplishing them, in order to gain their objective. "Leadership of the masses and drawing them into active revolutionary struggle demands that Communists have the ability to determine the main link in the chain of revolutionary events...."[18]

A good example of a "form of struggle" and a "main link" is provided by the Communists in their takeover of most of the countries in Eastern Europe following World War II.

After a dialectical analysis of the correlation of forces they determined that a coalition government would be the primary form of struggle. They also decided that the main link in the chain of revolutionary events would be for a Marxist-Leninist to be the Minister of the Interior in the coalition government. Note that the main link was not to have a Communist as head of the coalition government, but to have a Communist as Minister of the Interior, because he controlled the police. By controlling the police, the Communists were able to get rid of most of the influential anti-Communists. Control of the police was followed by the second most important link, or sequential step, control of the propaganda media. This was essential in confusing and dividing the opposition; destroying confidence in non-Communist institutions and leaders, and generally increasing discontent and antagonism against the existing governments. Control of the propaganda media was followed by the third sequential link, control of the economic structure. This made it possible for the Communists to control the rest of the populace since it gave them a virtual monopoly on commercial activity and employment. With control of these three power levers they had achieved their key and sequential objectives, and hence, were in a position to utilize them in gaining their strategic objective—control of national power.

Fourth, they keep the total dialectical situation under constant review and if there are significant changes in the correlation of forces, without hesitation or concern for apparent inconsistency, they will change the form of struggle, the main link, or the sequential steps, in order to cope with new problems or to take advantage of new weaknesses.

Specific Issues

Having discussed the Marxist-Leninists fundamental beliefs, objectives, ethics and morals and strategy and tactics, this section will be devoted to a number of specific questions which will provide more light on the nature of the problem we face. You will note that many of the answers will contain quotations from authoritative Communist figures and sources which further confirm that the nature of the Communist threat is as it has been described.

Q. Do the Soviets use the Marxist-Leninist method of planning to determine their foreign policies throughout the world?

A. Andrei Gromyko, Foreign Minister of the Soviet Union for 28 years, provides an answer to this question: "True to Lenin's precept on the party's role in sharing and implementing the foreign policy activity of the socialist state, the CPSU, its Central Committee, and the Central Committee Politburo routinely keep questions of Foreign Policy and international life in sight. They draw up and direct the foreign policy course of the USSR based on an in-depth Marxist-Leninist analysis of the situation in the international arena, and a correct estimation of the correlation of forces in the world and of the laws and factors which determine the chief trends and prospects of world development."[19]

In addition, a publication of the Communist Party of the Soviet Union says: "Our party is ever true to Marxism-Leninism and to its international duty; for more than half a century, the Soviet Union, guided by its Leninist Party, has been opposing imperialism in political, economic, ideological and military respects, and persistently and stubbornly building communism on the basis of Marxist-Leninist science. The Communist Party of the Soviet Union directs all its activity toward insuring that the world of socialism will be stronger today than yesterday, and stronger tomorrow than today. This task is being solved by the Soviet Union together with the other socialist countries. Together with them, the Soviet Union is helping and will help with all available means the revolutionary movement and all democratic and national liberation forces in their anti-imperialist struggle."[20]

Q. When the Communists were fighting us in Vietnam, were they using the Marxist-Leninist theory and guides to planning and action?

A.   The answer to this question is found in North Vietnamese General Giap's explanation of the basic reasons for their "victory": "Our strength is the strength of a heroic nation, the strength of the tradition of determination to fight and win....The great victory of our people also stems from the fully correct and very creative revolutionary and military line of our party. This line is actually the Marxist-Leninist theory ingenuously applied to the realities of Vietnam."[21] "..Our people with our party's correct revolutionary line and correct line of international solidarity based on Marxism-Leninism and proletarian internationalism—have been making positive contributions to the common cause of world revolution. Simultaneously, our people have been receiving increasingly great aid from the Soviet Union, China, and other fraternal socialist countries and enjoying active support from the progressive people of the entire world, including the American people."[22]

Q. Are the Chinese Communists still dedicated to Marxism-Leninism or have they "dumped Marx on the ash heap" as some of the media have reported?

A.   They are still dedicated to Marxism-Leninism. Deng Xiaoping has said: "What we uphold and must regard as the guide for our action is the basic principles of Marxism-Leninism—Mao Tse-Tung Thought, or the scientific system formed by these principles. As for individual theses, there are bound to be flaws, whether they come from Marx-Lenin or Mao Tse-Tung. However, such things do not come under the category of the scientific system formed by their basic principles....Scientific socialism forges ahead in the course of actual struggle, and so does Marxism-Leninism—Mao Tse-Tung Thought."[23]

In addition, Article 24 of the new constitution of the "People's Republic of China," (Adopted and promulgated 4 December 1982) says that the state "...educates the people in patriotism, internationalism and communism and in dialectical and historical materialism; it combats capitalist, feudal and other decadent ideas."[24]

("Mao Tse-Tung Thought is the application and development of Marxism-Leninism in China and is part of the scientific ideology of Marxism....Mao Tse-Tung Thought is not the Thought of Comrade Mao Tse-Tung himself. Instead it is the crystallization of the collective wisdom of the CCP. It has been acquired through the efforts of a large number of martyrs and revolutionaries in arduous struggle, bloodshed and sacrifice....Comrade Mao Tse-Tung is the most outstanding example of those who successfully applied Marxism in solving China's practical problems. He played an important part in founding and summarizing this ideology. Thus we call this ideology Mao Tse-Tung Thought."[25])

Q. Whenever we enter into negotiations with the Communists, the question is always asked, can we trust them? Can we?

A. The answer to this question can be found in the following quotations which define Communist ethics and morals:

"In what sense do we repudiate ethics and morality? In the sense that it is preached by the bourgeoisie, who derived ethics from God's Commandments. We, of course, say that we do not believe in God....

"We say that our morality is entirely subordinated to the interests of the class struggle of the proletariat. Our morality is derived from the interests of the class struggle of the proletariat....We say: 'morality is what serves to destroy the old exploiting society....' "[26]

"Ethical is that attitude which furthers the advance towards communism, while anything that impedes the advance is regarded as being unethical and amoral."[27]

Q. Whenever there is a change in Communist leadership there are always questions as to whether Communist policies may change. Is there a general answer to this question?

A. The general answer is that, as long as the leaders are Marxist-Leninists, there will be no change in their objectives, or ethics and morals, or method of planning. Changes will occur only if the new leadership believes new policies will be more effective in destroying non-Communist ways of life and establishing world Communism.

Q. Some say the Soviet Union is pursuing the same foreign policy objectives as the czars. What do the Marxist-Leninists say about this?

A.   "Whoever has mastered Marxist doctrine and understands the historic mission of the proletariat that Marx discovered is bound to be an internationalist, to strive consciously for the unity and cooperation of the working people of all nations, and to place the common interests of the international working class above partial, local and narrow national interests....

"Without internationalism, without the united efforts of the workers of all countries, it is impossible to defeat the world bourgeoisie and build a new society."[28]

"Proletarian internationalism, Lenin teaches, demands indivisibly, linking up the interests of the proletarian struggle in one country with the interests of this struggle in other countries, with the interests of the international working-class movement as a whole."[29]

Q.   Is a world Socialist/Communist revolution underway at this time?

A.   Yes. The Marxist-Leninists believe we are currently living in the era of "Imperialism," when "the world capitalist system as a whole is ripe for the social revolution of the proletariat."[30]

"The socialist revolution is not a single act nor a single battle. It is a whole era of class battles, economic, political and ideological. Lenin showed that the revolution would consist of a series of battles waged against the ruling classes by all the oppressed and discontented classes, group and elements of the population, but first and foremost by the proletariat and its ally, the peasantry."[31]

"...in our time, as Lenin taught, the world socialist revolution represents the joining of a great number of socialist, anti-imperialist, national liberation, general democratic, and other revolutions."[32]

"The national liberation movement against imperialism weakens and undermines it, thereby facilitating its overthrow by the workers of the more advanced countries. On the other hand, the workers' revolutionary struggle makes for the success of the national liberation struggle."[33]

"The Communist movement is an enormous political force: Marxist-Leninist parties exist in all continents—practically in every country where there is a working class. They operate under the most varied conditions, and therefore different approaches to various problems or differences of views on certain questions can appear among them. However, this does not hinder the joint struggle by Communists of various countries against the common adversary, and for the common objectives of the Communist movement. For the international duty of Marxist-Leninist parties consists of placing the common interests of the international workers movement above everything else and of effecting the closest fraternal cooperation in the struggle for common objectives."[34]

"The Communist and workers' parties are conducting their activity in diverse specific conditions, requiring an appropriate approach to the solution of concrete problems. Each party, guided by the principles of Marxism-Leninism and in keeping with concrete national conditions, fully independent, elaborates its own policy, determines the directions, forms and methods of struggle and, depending on the circumstance, chooses the peaceful or non-peaceful way of transition to socialism...."[35]

"Conscious of its internationalist duty, the Communist party of the Soviet Union will continue to pursue a line in international affairs that facilitates a further step-up in the activity of the worldwide anti-imperialist struggle and the strengthening of the combat unity of all its participants.

"The complete triumph of the cause of socialism is inevitable. We shall spare no efforts in the struggle for this triumph."[36]

Q. What kinds of actions are the Communists taking within the United States?

A.   Mr. Edward O'Malley, Assistant Director of the Federal Bureau of Investigation has described the objectives of Soviet "active measures" in the United States as follows:

"The basic aims of Soviet active measures are to weaken the opponents of the USSR and to create a favorable environment for the promotion of Soviet views and Soviet foreign policy objectives. The Kremlin continues to view the United States as the 'main enemy,' and most active measures are directed against American policies or American interests throughout the world.

"Although specific objectives and tactics of Soviet active measures in the United States may vary in accordance with the changing world situation, they have certain long-range strategic objectives:

- Articulate and promote Soviet views and positions on foreign policy issues;
- Seek support for Soviet policy interests in all strata of American Society (particularly political, business, academic, journalistic, and 'progressive or activist' circles);
- Reinforce and mobilize domestic opposition to United States Government policies that are considered inimical to Soviet interests;
- Promulgate justifications for Soviet actions at home and abroad;

- Portray Soviet government, society, and culture in a favorable manner.

"Recent KGB active measures operations in the United States have focused on arms control and disarmament matters, and the peace movement. Specific Soviet objectives are to promote Soviet views on intermediate-range nuclear force (INF), negotiations and strategic arms reduction talks (START), and to support and reinforce domestic opposition to Reagan Administration defense policies and budget, as well as the production and/or deployment of Pershing II and cruise missiles in Western Europe, enhanced radiation weapons or 'neutron bomb,' MX missile, and the B-1 bomber."[37]

Mr. O'Malley also described specific kinds of Soviet global active measures:

"Active measures include a wide range of activities, including the following:

Manipulation or control of the media;

Written or oral disinformation;

Forgeries;

Use of foreign Communist parties and international front organizations;

Clandestine radio broadcasting;

Economic warfare;

Military and paramilitary operations;

Political influence operations utilizing agents of influence, manipulation of private communication channels, and exploitation of unwitting contacts; and

Covert propaganda."[38]

Former Senator Paula Hawkins, when Chairman of the Senate Drug Enforcement Caucus, described an action developed by another Communist country, Cuba:

"The fact that Castro has chosen to associate himself with criminal elements and international drug smugglers, I believe, is a clear indication of his contempt for international law and his intent to undermine American society through drug addiction, moral corruption and violent crime. Investigations reveal that the Cuban dictator's support of drug trafficking is linked to his promotion of terrorism in Latin America. Ships are loaded with drugs in Cuba to be taken to the United States. They leave the United States. Many of these ships return to Cuba with weapons destined for the South American mainland."[39]

Q. What is the nature of the Communist threat in Central America?

A.   This is best answered by reviewing Che Guevara's conclusions concerning revolutions in the Americas, and excerpts from S. A. Mikoyen's analysis of the Communist takeover in Nicaragua.

First, Che Guevara: "We believe that the Cuban revolution revealed three fundamental conclusions about armed revolution in the Americas. (1) Popular forces can win a war against an army; (2) One does not have to wait for a revolutionary situation to arise, it can be created; (3) In the underdeveloped countries of the Americas, rural areas are the best battlefields for revolution."[40] S. A. Mikoyen: "The Nicaraguan revolution undoubtedly belongs among the events which will force us to review certain well established concepts....There is not a single example of a victorious revolution carried out peacefully on the continent....As yet only the armed path has led to the victory of revolutions in Latin America. And the Nicaraguan experience confirms what had been considered refuted by some, after the death of Che Guevara and the defeat of a number of other guerrilla movements....A seriously and scientifically understood armed path of revolution presupposes the obligatory use of the most diverse forms and methods of struggle including those which are usually considered inherent to the peaceful path.... The military-political fronts of the sort of the 'Movement of 26 July' in Cuba and the Sandinista National Liberation front (S.F.N.L.) in Nicaragua have shown (and now can be considered proven) that under certain conditions they are capable of taking over the political parties of the proletariat as a revolutionary vanguard. Fidel Castro, in one of his speeches, explained not only the possibility of such a phenomenon, but also its inevitability, or more accurately, the absence of any other possibility under the specific conditions of Cuba in the 1950s. A similar situation developed in Nicaragua in the 1960s and 1970s.... Providing a favorable international situation—the international situation should be composed of two basic components: in the first place, the receiving of support and aid in various forms, from the broadest circle of friends and allies; secondly, the isolating of opponents for the purpose of preventing direct intervention by them....It is difficult to assume that Nicaraguan events, right up to 19 July 1979, could have occurred before a decisive change in the balance of forces between the two world systems, before the victory of the Cuban revolution, and so forth. Since much has been written about this, let us merely take up in greater detail, the clearly apparent fact of the erosion of the O.A.S., as a punitive mechanism in the hands of United States Imperialism...."[41]

Q. Why are the Soviets continually strengthening their military capability and would they launch a surprise nuclear attack?

A. The Marxist-Leninist leaders of the Soviet Union are totally dedicated to spreading Communism over the Earth. They are developing a military capability beyond their legitimate needs for defense. It is apparent that they hope to build a military capability which will increase their ability to foment and support various categories of revolutions and to dissuade or discourage non-Communists from resisting these activities. Also they hope to develop such a military superiority that in future confrontations we and the other non-Communists, "realizing the hopelessness of resistance,"[42] will surrender to them without a fight.

Failing this bloodless victory they hope to have a military superiority that will let them prevail in a military conflict. They describe the nature of a future war as follows:

"It...will be a bitter armed clash between two diametrically opposed social systems, a struggle between two coalitions, the socialists and the imperialists, in which every side will pursue the most decisive aims.

"As regards the means used, this war may be a nuclear one. Even though nuclear weapons will play the decisive role in the war, final victory over the aggressor can be achieved only as a result of the joint actions of all the arms of the services, which must utilize in full measure the results of the nuclear strikes at the enemy and fulfill their specific tasks.

"As regards its scope the nuclear war will be a world war and an intercontinental one. This is determined both by its sociopolitical content and by the fact that both sides possess missiles of practically unlimited range, atomic missile-carrying submarines, and strategic bombers. The war will engulf practically the entire planet.

"It will be waged by methods differing radically from those used in the past. Formerly, the direct aim of all military actions was to rout the enemy's forces, without which it was impossible to reach vital strategic centers. Now the situation has changed. The use of nuclear missile weapons makes it possible to attain decisive military results in a very short time, at any distance, and on vast territories. In the event of war not only groupings of the enemy's armed forces will be subjected to destructive nuclear strikes, but also industrial and political centers, communication centers, everything that feeds the arteries of war.

"The first massive nuclear strikes are able largely to predetermine the subsequent course of the war...."[43]

"To attain the greatest effectiveness, it is recommended that the nuclear strikes be launched at the start of the fire preparation unexpectedly for the enemy. Preemption in launching a nuclear strike is considered to be the decisive condition for the attainment of superiority over him and the seizure and retention of the initiative."[44]

Certainly the Soviets would like to avoid the costs of nuclear war by achieving world Communism with revolution or by developing a military superiority that would cause us to capitulate without a fight. But there is nothing in Soviet ideology, morality, or strategy and tactics that would prevent them from launching a surprise nuclear attack if their dialectical analysis of the correlation of forces convincingly showed that the total gains of such an attack would be worth the total costs. In fact, they would be failing in their duty and violating their Communist morality if they did not do so.

Conclusions

The key to understanding and believing the true nature of the Communist problem is to understand Marxism-Leninism.

All Marxist-Leninists are dedicated to destroying all non-Communist ways of life throughout the world, using any and every means without moral constraint, as long as they believe the total gains will be worth the total costs.

Today, Marxist-Leninists control the governments and direct the lives of about one-third of the human race. In almost every other nation, where they are not in control, there are Marxist-Leninists working to eliminate non-Communist governments and to bring them under Communist domination. Every day of every year, in peace or in war, the Communists are insidiously waging an undeclared war of internal aggression against all non-Communist countries. The focus of their efforts is to cause people to lose confidence in non-Communist institutions, policies and leaders, to increase discontent and antagonisms, and generally to reduce non-Communist will and capability to resist.

The Communists achieve their objectives by identifying, developing, and exploiting weakness. They do not have just military defense departments; in effect they have ideological, psychological, economic, political, diplomatic and military offense departments.

All Marxist-Leninists, throughout the world, use a four-step method of analysis and planning to identify existing and potential areas of weakness and to determine the best way to exploit them. The plans and actions that result from this method of planning are confusing to non-Marxist-Leninists because, while the Communists' ultimate objectives and ethics and morals are constant, their actions in the various countries do not follow a standard pattern. They are responsive to specific situations, issues and weaknesses in each country.

While the Communists have declared their intention to seize power and impose Marxist-Leninist rule on every country in the world, they do not openly "declare war" against specific countries. They just start what can be described as termite operations. Like termites, they gnaw away at the strength of non-Communist structures. In individual nations these termite operations are a form of conspiratorial internal aggression, spearheaded by native Marxist-Leninist "termites" who are nurtured from the main "nests," the countries already under Marxist-Leninist control. In these termite operations the native Marxist-Leninists use ideological, psychological and political forms of struggle in efforts to confuse and divide the non-Communists and cause them to lose confidence in their non-Communist institutions, policies and leaders. Economically and militarily they work to weaken the non-Communists' capability and will to resist the Communists. When the Communists use force, beyond terrorism, such as guerilla warfare, the termite operations continue.

Like all Marxist-Leninists throughout the world, the Marxist-Leninist leaders of the Soviet Union are totally dedicated to spreading Communism over the Earth. They are developing a military capability beyond their legitimate needs for defense. At the same time that they are building their strength, they are using various forms of struggle to weaken the will and capability of the non-Communist world to resist. This includes such things as: supporting any revolutionary activity, even those led by anti-Communists, if they believe it will result in our being denied essential raw materials, strategic position or otherwise weakened; trying to break up remaining non-Communist collective defense arrangements like NATO and ANZUS; trying to get us to agree to nuclear free zones, or a nuclear freeze or a disarmament agreement that will lessen our ability to deter them from attempting coercion or from trying to take us by the "scruff of the neck." It is apparent that they hope to build a military capability which will increase their ability to foment and support various categories of revolutions and to dissuade or discourage non-Communists from resisting these activities. Also they hope to develop such a military superiority that in future confrontations we and the other non-Communists, "realizing the hopelessness of resistance," will surrender to them without a fight.

Certainly the Soviets would like tó avoid the costs of nuclear war by

118

achieving world Communism with revolution or by developing a military superiority that would cause us to capitulate without a fight. But there is nothing in Soviet ideology, morality, or strategy and tactics that would prevent them from launching a surprise nuclear attack if their dialectical analysis of the correlation of forces convincingly showed that the total gains of such an attack would be worth the total costs. In fact, they would be failing in their duty and violating their Communist morality if they did not do so.

Appropriate Actions

There are many actions that should be taken to prevent the Communists from achieving their objectives. But at this point in time the most needed actions are those which will lead to a worldwide understanding of the true nature of the Communist threat. If there was such an understanding, all non-Communist nations would realize that the common deadly threat made them natural allies.

Knowing Communist objectives, ethics and morals and method of analysis and planning, should prompt them to join together in developing organizations and procedures which would make it possible for them to determine areas of weakness the Communists would likely try to exploit. Action could then be taken to stop or prevent indirect or direct aggression, and at the lowest possible levels of cost and involvement.

Probably the best way to start achieving the needed understanding of the Communist threat would be for the President of the United States to appoint a bipartisan committee to develop a paper setting forth the fundamental beliefs, objectives, ethics and morals, and strategy and tactics of Marxist-Leninists throughout the world.

This paper would then be submitted to Congress as a proposed concurrent resolution expressing the sense of the Congress. Hopefully, the resulting debate and finally approved version would be covered by national and international television and the other media.

Following publication of the sense-of-the-Congress resolution a prime time type television documentary, depicting the contents of the resolution, should be made and shown to the American public and throughout the world.

There is a second thing we should do to improve our batting average in preventing the Marxist-Leninists from seizing power in additional countries. We should borrow their method of analysis and planning and use it as they do. This would enable us to determine in advance the likely weaknesses they will try to exploit; the likely "forms of struggle" they will use; and the likely actions they will take.

We could then take actions to prevent Communist successes before the situation in a country deteriorates to the point (as it has in the past) that we have only two choices, let it go Communist, or step in to prevent it at great cost.

We can establish such a capability by initiating some new interdepartment and interagency requirements and procedures, within existing components of our government. Essentially the structure and procedures could be something like this: (1) The "country teams" in our embassies throughout the world are staffed with people from a number of United States departments and agencies. Collectively, they have specialized understandings in many areas, ideological, sociological, political, economic, diplomatic and military. These understandings will enable the "country teams" in each country to periodically make a Communist style total dialectical analysis of the correlation of forces within and acting upon the countries where they are stationed. (2) Then on the basis of this analysis, their understanding of Communist objectives, ethics and morals, strategy and tactics, and communist capabilities, they can estimate the likely weaknesses the Communists will try to exploit, the forms of struggle they will likely use, the "key link" and the probable sequence of actions they will take to achieve their objectives. (3) Using the understandings provided by these estimates, and consistent with our national values, interests, commitments and capabilities, the "country team" could develop recommended policies, plans and actions designed to eliminate critical weaknesses, before the Communists can exploit them. (4) These recommended policies, plans and actions, together with their dialectical analysis, would then be sent to each department and agency concerned, for consideration by appropriate experts who would have a short specified time to concur in the policies, plans and actions, or to recommend additions, deletions or changes. (5) The departments and agencies would then submit their concurrences or recommended changes to the National Security Council staff. The National Security Council staff would have a short specified time to: Attempt to resolve the differences between departments and agencies; meet with appropriate representatives of the departments and agencies to consider regional and global implications; then prepare the agreed recommended policies, plans and actions, the agreed regional and global implications; together with a listing of the unresolved differences, and forward them to the president for his decisions.

To the extent that we develop a generally agreed understanding of the true nature of the Communist threat we can be sure that "we the people" of the United States, and the other non-Communists throughout the world, will support the policies and plans necessary to prevent further Communist expansion.

If we borrow the Communists method of analysis and planning, and use it as they do, we can develop policies and plans that will prevent the Communists from seizing additional countries; and do so at the lowest levels of cost and involvement.

If we do these things, we can be sure that self-determinations, and not Communist domination, will shape the future ways of life of the human race.

[1]L.I. Brezhnev, *On The Policy Of The Soviet Union and The International Situation* (Prepared by the Novosti Press Agency Publishing House, Moscow), (Garden City, New York: Doubleday and Company, Inc., 1973), p. 18.

[2]*Fundamentals of Marxism-Leninism* (Moscow: Foreign Language Publishing House, 1963), p. 21.

[3]*The Road to Communism* (Moscow: Foreign Languages Publishing House, 1961), p. 454.

[4]*History Of The Communist Party Soviet Union* (Moscow: Foreign Languages Publishing House, Second Revised Edition), p. 729.

[5]*V. I. Lenin, Selected Works* (New York: International Publishers, 1943), Vol. X, p. 337.

[6]V. I. Lenin, "Left Wing Communism," as printed in *A Handbook of Marxism* (New York: International Publishers, 1935), p. 859.

[7]*Marxism-Leninism On War And Army*, (Moscow: Progress Publishers, 1972), p. 385.

[8]V. I. Lenin, *Collected Works*, Russian Edition, Vol. X, pp. 80-81; Quoted in *Strategy And Tactics Of The Proletarian Revolution*, (New York: International Publishers, 1936), p. 30.

[9]From the text of the main document adopted by an international meeting of 75 Communist and Workers Parties in Moscow on June 17, 1969. As translated in U.S. Govt. F.B.I.S. *Daily Report On The Soviet Union*, June 18, 1969, p. A-21.

[10]V. I. Lenin, *Selected Works*, Vol. VII, (New York: International Publishers, 1943), p. 357.

[11]*Ibid.*, Vol. VIII, p. 282.

[12]V. I. Lenin, *Collected Works*, Russian Edition, Vol. X, Quoted in

Strategy And Tactics Of The Proletarian Revolution, (New York: International Publishers, 1936), p. 57.

[13]*Fundamentals of Marxism-Leninism,* (Foreign Languages Publishing House, Moscow, 1963), p. 502.

[14]V. I. Lenin, as quoted in *History of The Communist Party of The Soviet Union,* (Foreign Languages Publishing House, Second Revised Edition, not dated), p. 200.

[15]V. I. Lenin, *Selected Works,* Vol. VIII, (New York: International Publishers, 1943), pp. 279-280.

[16]*Ibid.,* Vol. X, p. 112.

[17]*Ibid.,* pp. 169-170.

[18]V. V. Zagladin, Editor, *The International Communist Movement: Sketch Of Strategy And Tactics,* Part I, (Moscow Political Literature Publishing House, 1972), translated by U.S. Department of Commerce, Joint Publications Research Service, Arlington, Virginia, p. 25.

[19]Andrei Gromyko, "Leninist Foreign Policy In The Contemporary World," *Kommunist #1,* (Moscow, January 1981), p. 13.

[20]*Kommunist #10,* (Moscow, 10 July 1969), pp. 20-31.

[21]General Vo Nguyen Giap, as quoted in U.S. Govt. F.B.I.S., *Daily Report, North Vietnam,* (December 23, 1968), p. K 6.

[22]General Vo Nguyen Giap, *Ibid.,* 13 February 1970, p. 11.

[23]Deng Xiaoping, as quoted in the U.S. Government Foreign Broadcast Information Service (F.B.I.S.), China, *PRC NATIONAL AFFAIRS,* (3 November 1981), p. K 3.

[24]*Fifth Session of The Fifth National People's Congress (Main Documents),* (Foreign Languages Press, BEIJING, 1983), p. 19.

[25]Lu Zhichao, as quoted in the U.S. Government F.B.I.S., China, *PRC NATIONAL AFFAIRS* (14 September 1981), p. K 17.

[26]V. I. Lenin, "The Tasks of the Youth Leagues," *Marx, Engels, Marxism* (Foreign Language Publishing House, Moscow, 1947), pp. 461-463.

[27]V. Afanasyev, *Socialism And Communism,* (Progress Publishers, Moscow, 1972), p. 175.

[28]*Fundamentals of Marxism-Leninism,* (Foreign Languages Publishing House, Moscow, 1963), p. 305.

[29]*History of The Communist Party of The Soviet Union,* (Foreign Languages Publishing House, Moscow, Second Revised Edition, not dated), p. 757.

[30]*The International Communist Movement: Sketch of Strategy And Tactics,* (Textbook for Party Education, Edited by V.V. Zagladin, Second Edition, Revised and Supplemented. Political Literature Publishing House,

Moscow, 14 January 1972), p. 15.

[31]*History of The Communist Party of The Soviet Union*, p. 198.

[32]*The International Communist Movement*, p. 18.

[33]*History of The Communist Party of The Soviet Union*, p. 198.

[34]*Kommunist #7*, Signed To Press 6 May 1969, Moscow. As quoted in U.S. Government F.B.I.S., (Publication on USSR International Affairs, 29 May 1969), p. 42.

[35]From the text of the main document adopted by an international meeting of 75 Communist and Workers Parties in Moscow on June 17, 1969. As translated in U.S. Government F.B.I.S. *Daily Report on The Soviet Union*, 18 June 1969, p. A-21.

[36]L. I. Brezhnev, *24th Congress of The Communist Party of The Soviet Union Stenographic Report (Part 1)*, as translated by the U.S. Government Joint Publications Research Service, Arlington, Virginia, 1971, p. 41.

[37]Edward O'Malley, *Hearings Before The Permanent Select Committee on Intelligence*, House of Representatives, July 13-14, 1982, (U.S. Government Printing Office, Washington, D.C., 1982), pp. 220-221.

[38]*Ibid.*

[39]Paula Hawkins, *Joint Hearing Before The Subcommittee on Security and Terrorism of The Committee on The Judiciary and The Subcommittee on Western Hemisphere Affairs of The Foreign Relations Committe and The Senate Drug Enforcement Caucus, United States Senate*, April 30, 1983, (U.S. Government Printing Office, Washington, D.C., 1983), p. 3.

[40]Che Guevara, *Guerilla Warfare*, (Frederick Praeger Publisher, New York, 1962), pp. 3-4.

[41]S. A. Mikoyen, *On The Particular Features of The Revolution in Nicaragua and Its Lessons From The Viewpoint of The Theory and Practice of The Liberation Movement (Concluding Statement)*, (Latinskaya Amerika, Moscow, March 1980), pp. 34-44.

[42]*Fundamentals of Marxism-Leninism*, (Foreign Languages Publishing House, Moscow, 1963), p. 502.

[43]*Marxism-Leninism on War and Army*, (Progress Publishers, Moscow, 1972), published under the auspices of the United States Air Force, p. 304.

[44]A. A. Sidorenko, *The Offensive* (Moscow, 1970), translated and published under the auspices of the United States Air Force, p. 115.